SIGNPOST

SELECTED PREMIER HOTELS 2015

www.signpost.co.uk

SIGNPOST 2015

Welcome to the 76th edition of Signpost, the UK's longest established annual guide to the country's premier hotels.

The Signpost Guide to Selected Premier Hotels has been published almost every year since 1935 and while a few things may have changed in recent years, including the ways in which visitors appraise and select places to stay, Signpost's values remain very much the same as they have always been. We use our knowledge and experience to select and inspect only the best quality hotels, so that you can book with confidence and know that your stay will be exceptional.

To join the Signpost Selected Premier Hotels collection, potential member hotels, which are usually small and proprietor-run, must offer exceptional style, a personal welcome, good cuisine and the very best in guest care. Most have lots to see and do nearby too. We stay at each hotel at least once in every three years, or we sample the restaurant and make a thorough inspection so that whichever Signpost hotel you choose, you can rest assured it meets the highest standards.

Find your perfect hotel using the Features Index in the back of the book, where you can see locations and special facilities at a glance. Or, if you have a specific hotel in mind, use the alphabetical index to find it in the book. Don't forget to keep checking our website **www.signpost.co.uk** for more information and hotel reviews. You can also subscribe online to our newsletter to receive special offers throughout the year.

We wish all our readers and hotel members a happy and successful year and remember, wherever you are in the UK, look out for the **new** Signpost sign – our stamp of approval and your guarantee of a top quality stay.

We know you'll love staying at our hotels and we'd love you to invite your friends and family to experience a break in a Signpost hotel. Contact us at **enquiries@signpost.co.uk** to purchase Gift Vouchers today. Vouchers are available in denominations of £50 and £100 and make a wonderful present.

SCOTLAND

NORTH EAST

YORKSHIRE

NORTH WEST

EAST MIDLANDS

HEART OF ENGLAND

EAST OF ENGLAND

WALES

LONDON

SOUTH EAST

SOUTH WEST

CHOOSE A REGION

See the map of regions on page 2. To browse the hotels in a particular region, simply turn to the matching colour coded section. Alternatively, you can use the colour maps starting on page 177 to locate a specific hotel. Page numbers for each Signpost hotel in this book are shown on the maps.

SELECT A HOTEL

Choose from a wide range of Signpost hotels in each region. Each page features a different hotel, with colour photographs and a description to help give you an idea of the hotel's character and its surrounding attractions. You will also find quick glance information on the hotel's facilities.

HOW TO BOOK A HOTEL

ONLINE:

Go to **www.signpost.co.uk** to make a reservation at your chosen Signpost hotel. Remember to check the Signpost website and subscribe to our newsletter for special offers.

BY PHONE:

You can also book a room by phoning the number on the hotel's page.

CONTENTS

INFORMATION ABOUT MANY OF THE ACCOMMODATION SERVICES AND FACILITIES IS GIVEN IN THE FORM OF SYMBOLS.

Site Features

- **P** Private parking
- Garden
- € Euros accepted
- Visa/Mastercard/Switch accepted

Leisure Facilities

- Tennis court(s)
- Swimming pool – outdoor
- Swimming pool – indoor
- Sauna on site
- Health/beauty facilities on site
- Gym on site
- Games room
- Riding/pony-trekking nearby
- Golf available (on site or nearby)
- Fishing nearby
- Cycles for hire nearby

Property Facilities

- Real log/coal fires
- Passenger lift
- Night porter
- Lounge for residents' use
- Laundry facilities
- WiFi or internet access

Dogs/pets accepted by arrangement
- Conference facilities
- Air conditioning

Children

- High chairs available
- Cots available
- Children welcome

Catering

- Special diets available
- Licenced (table or bar)
- Evening meals

Room Facilities

- DVD player
- Television
- Satellite/cable/freeview TV
- Telephone
- Tea/coffee making in bedrooms
- Hairdryer
- Bedrooms on ground floor
- Four-poster bed(s)
- Smoking rooms available

Campus/Hostels

- Cooking facilities available

Many Hotels have a star rating from one of the four assessing bodies – VisitEngland, VisitScotland, Visit Wales or the AA, which are shown on accommodation entries.

Accommodation entries may also show Gold, Silver, or other awards given in recognition of exceptional quality.

VisitEngland's Breakfast Award recognises hotels and B&Bs that offer a high quality choice of breakfast, service and hospitality that exceeds what would be expected at their star rating.

Pets Come Too - accommodation displaying this symbol offer a special welcome to pets. Please check for any restrictions before booking.

Businesses displaying this logo have undergone a recognised verification process to ensure that they are sustainable (green).

Welcome Schemes

These symbols identify businesses that belong to recognised Walkers, Cyclists, Families and Pets Welcome schemes.

HOTEL FACILITIES

Unless stated otherwise ALL Signpost hotels have:

- direct dial telephones
- colour TV
- tea/coffee making
- en-suite bathrooms
- hairdryers
- laundry service

SYMBOLS are printed where there are other unique facilities at hotels. Symbols for golf, fishing, shooting or riding denote that these activities can be arranged near to the Signpost hotel.

HIGHLIGHTS

In each regional section you will find a selection of historic houses, gardens and places of interest to visit during your stay at your Signpost hotel.

These sites are recommended by Hudson's Historic Houses and Gardens.

Visit **www.hudsonsheritage.com** to find more places to enjoy on your holiday and details of special events.

ACCOMMODATION ENTRIES EXPLAINED

Each accommodation entry contains detailed information to help you decide if it is right for you. This has been provided by proprietors and our aim is to ensure that it is as objective and factual as possible.

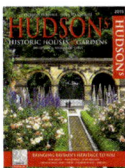

HOLBECK GHYLL COUNTRY HOUSE HOTEL

Cumbria - Windermere

BEDROOMS: 27
Bedrooms contain decanters of locally-distilled damson gin, fresh flowers, luxurious Egyptian cotton sheets and robes, private terraces and hot tubs.

B&B PER ROOM PER NIGHT:
S: £150.00 - £245.00
D: £170.00 - £390.00

ADDITIONAL INFORMATION:
The boutique Spa, with sauna, steam room and heated outdoor hot tub features stunning views across to the Langdales Pikes and Coniston Old Man, perfect for relaxing into at the end of the day.

Holbeck Lane, Windermere, Cumbria LA23 1LU
T: (01539) 432375 F: (01539) 434743
E: stay@holbeckghyll.com W: www.holbeckghyll.com

Holbeck is more like a beautiful private home than a hotel, with no two of our richly-appointed rooms the same. Whether you choose to sink into an armchair by the inglenook fireplace with the morning's newspaper, or rest your fell-weary limbs in one of the sumptuous lounges overlooking the Lake District in all its glory, you'll find the perfect spot to recharge your batteries. There are 13 beautiful rooms and suites in the main house, 6 exquisite rooms in The Lodge, 3 luxury cottages, 4 fabulous suites and our splendid Miss Potter suite where Hollywood star Renée Zellweger lived during filming of the movie about Beatrix Potter's life. Bedrooms enjoy an intoxicating view over Windermere that has been voted among the top 15 in the world.

DINING: The head chef David McLaughlin, has built a reputation around serving the very finest ingredients.

Payment: Leisure: Property: Children: Catering: Room:

1. County and town
2. Pet friendly facilities
3. Establishment name
4. Room information
5. Ratings and awards
6. Prices per room per night for bed and breakfast
7. Additional information
8. At-a-glance facility symbols
9. Dining information
10. Contact details

OUR STANDARDS

Signpost is the UK's longest established colour accommodation guide and is now in its 76th year of publication. The high standards set by the founders of Signpost, remain today. Every year, our inspectors personally visit each Signpost hotel to ensure that the expected standards are met. Each hotel is inspected according to the following criteria:

• Individual style,
• Good value, friendly service
• A personal welcome

Our inspectors expect the finest cuisine, using the best fresh produce. The bedrooms in a Signpost hotel must be furnished with style and offer all the comforts of a home from home. Signpost hotels are located in appealing, fascinating areas, with plenty of available sporting and leisure activities.

Most importantly, a Signpost hotel is a place you will want to visit again and again.

LOOK OUT FOR THE NEW SIGNPOST SIGN YOUR GUARANTEE OF A TOP QUALITY HOTEL

SIGNPOST
H O T E L S

Gloucestershire

Wiltshire

Somerset

Devon   Dorset

Cornwall

Channel Islands

SOUTH WEST
Cornwall & Isles of Scilly, Devon, Dorset, Gloucestershire, Somerset, Wiltshire, Channel Islands

A spectacular combination of ancient countryside and glorious coastline, Britain's South West is its most popular holiday area. It stretches from the soft stone and undulating hills of the Cotswolds in the north, through Wiltshire with its historic monuments, to the wild moors, turquoise waters, golden sands and pretty harbours of Dorset, Devon and Cornwall. The beauty of this region and all it has to offer never fails to delight.

SOUTH WEST

CORNWALL

Spectacular turquoise seas and white sands dotted with fishing harbours, beautiful gardens and the remnants of Cornwall's fascinating industrial heritage draw visitors from far and wide. The pounding waves to be found along the coastline attract surfers from all over to the world famous beaches around Newquay and make Cornwall a mecca for watersports enthusiasts of all kinds.

The majestic and largely untouched wilderness of Bodmin Moor is only one example of the rich natural environment that can be found here, with miles of walking paths criss-crossing the impressive landscape and offering panoramic views. This captivating scenery continues to intrigue and inspire a vibrant art scene centred around St Ives. The county has a diverse history with prehistoric, Celtic and medieval roots and a huge number of heritage attractions to choose from. Tintagel Castle overlooks the dramatic windswept Atlantic coast, and the Grade I listed Port Eliot House & Gardens is a hidden gem nestling beside a secret estuary near Saltash.

Eden Project
St. Austell, Cornwall PL24 2SG
(01726) 811911
www.edenproject.com
Explore your relationship with nature at the world famous Eden Project. Be inspired by cutting-edge buildings, stunning year round garden displays, world-class sculpture and art, as well as fabulous music and arts events. See all the sights and immerse yourself in nature with a walk among the treetops on the Rainforest Canopy Walk or a ride on the land train.

DEVON

Take a hike or a mountain bike and discover the rugged beauty of Exmoor, explore the drama of the craggy coastline, or take a boat trip from a pretty harbour. North Devon is also rich in heritage with stately homes and attractions including Hartland Abbey and the picturesque Clovelly village.

Stunningly beautiful, Dartmoor is perhaps the most famous of Devon's National Parks and offers miles of purple, heather-clad moorland, rushing rivers and stone tors. Walk the length and breadth of the moor or cycle the Drake's Trail, where you'll come across wild ponies and plenty of moorland pubs, perfect for a well earned rest. Head east and discover the imposing Blackdown Hills Area of Outstanding Natural Beauty, stopping off in one of the area's picture-postcard villages for a delicious Devon Cream Tea.

Plymouth is famous for its seafaring heritage, with Plymouth

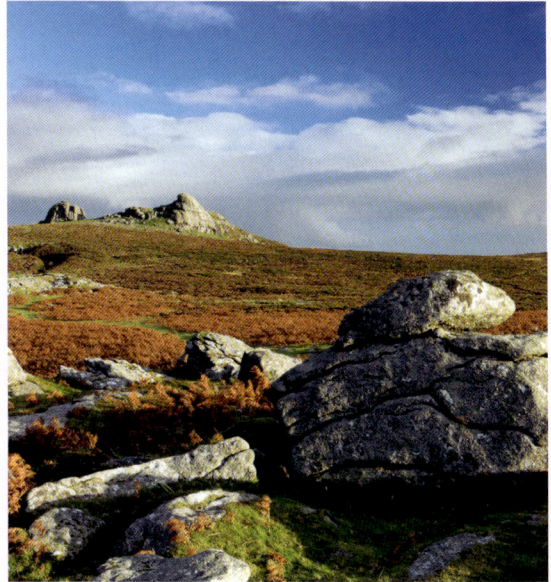

Hoe as the backdrop for Sir Francis Drake's legendary game of bowls, as well as being one of the most beautiful natural harbours in the world. Climb Smeaton's Tower for the incredible views if you're feeling energetic, or visit the world-famous Plymouth Gin Distillery at Sutton Harbour.

Torquay, gateway to the English Riviera, boasts elegant Victorian villas, iconic palm trees, a sweeping sandy beach and a rich maritime history. Paignton offers great days out including its famous zoo, and the traditional fishing harbour of Brixham is awash with seafood restaurants, waterside pubs and cafés. This whole area is also home to a huge selection of beaches from small, romantic coves to larger, award-winning stretches. The Jurassic Coast is a UNESCO World Heritage Site which stretches for 95 miles along the Devon/Dorset coast, revealing 185 million years of geology and is a must for visitors to the South West.

DORSET

Stretching from historic Lyme Regis in the west to Christchurch in the east, and including a number of designated heritage areas, the whole Dorset coastline is a treasure trove of geology. Interesting landforms are plentiful - Durdle Door, Lulworth Cove, the Isle of Portland with the famous Portland Bill lighthouse and the shingle bank of Chesil Beach to name but a few. Weymouth and Portland are two of the best sailing locations in Europe and offer water sports galore, as well as pretty harbours. For traditional English seaside resorts visit Victorian Swanage, or Bournemouth with its fine sandy beach, perfect for families. Inland, enchanting market towns, quaint villages and rolling countryside play host to delightful shops, museums, family attractions, historic houses and beautiful gardens such as the Sub-Tropical Gardens at Abbotsbury. Explore Dorset's natural beauty on foot or by bicycle at Stoborough Heath and Hartland Moor nature reserves.

Sherborne Castle & Gardens
Sherborne, Dorset DT9 5NR
(01935) 812072
www.sherbornecastle.com
Built by Sir Walter Raleigh in c1594, the castle reflects various styles from the Elizabethan hall to the Victorian solarium, with splendid collections of art, furniture and porcelain. The grounds around the 50-acre lake were landscaped by 'Capability' Brown.

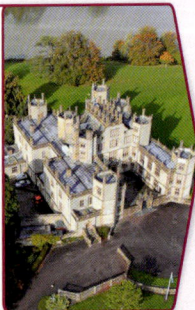

GLOUCESTERSHIRE

Perfect for a relaxing break or as a base for touring the Cotswolds, Cheltenham is an elegant spa town where Regency town houses line the historic promenade and leafy squares. Relax in award-winning gardens or visit one of the impressive range of sporting and cultural events such as The Cheltenham Gold Cup or The Cheltenham Festival of music.

In the north of the Severn Vale, the ancient settlement of Tewkesbury, famous for its fine half-timbered buildings, network of alleyways and 12th Century Norman Abbey, is one of the best medieval townscapes in England. Enjoy a riverside stroll along the River Severn or a boat trip along the Avon. At the centre of the Severn Vale, Gloucester is a vibrant and multicultural city, combining historic architecture with numerous visitor attractions, shops and a collection of mouth watering tea shops, restaurants, bars and pubs. The city, with its impressive cathedral, is linked to Sharpness Docks via the historic 16 mile ship canal and the ancient woodlands of Forest of Dean are only a stone's throw away.

SOMERSET & BRISTOL

The maritime city of Bristol is packed with historic attractions, exciting events and fabulous festivals. Cabot Circus offers first class shopping, while stylish restaurants and cafés on the Harbourside serve up locally produced food to tempt and delight. Out and about, Isambard Kingdom Brunel's Clifton Suspension Bridge and the Bristol Zoo Gardens are firm favourites.

Topped by the tower of the ruined 15th Century church, Glastonbury Tor is the stuff of myth and legend, rising high above the Somerset Levels near the delightful town of Glastonbury. Believed to be the site of a Saxon fortress, it has breathtaking views reaching to Wells, the Mendips and the Bristol Channel in the north, Shepton Mallet and Wiltshire in the east, south to the Polden Hills and to the Quantocks and Exmoor in the west.

Roman Bath
Bath, Somerset BA1 1LZ
(01225) 477785
www.romanbaths.co.uk
Bathe in the naturally hot spa water at the magnificent baths built by the romans, indulge in a gourmet getaway, or enjoy a romantic weekend exploring the wealth of historic architecture. You can find all of this in the beautiful city of Bath and attractions such as Longleat Safari Park and Stonehenge are all within easy reach too.

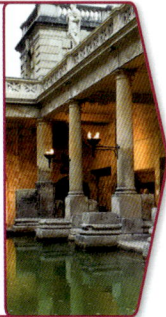

WILTSHIRE

Surrounded by stunning scenery and home to a magnificent Cathedral, a wealth of heritage, cultural, dining and shopping venues, the medieval city of Salisbury is the jewel in the crown of South West England's rural heartland.

Further afield you can find an abundance of quintessential English market towns including Chippenham, Devizes, and the county town of Trowbridge. Marlborough, famed for its charming high street and independent shops, is stylish and sophisticated with a cosmopolitan café culture, while Wilton, the ancient capital of Wessex, is home to Wilton House and a beautiful Italianate Church.

The Neolithic site of Stonehenge is one of the most famous megalithic monuments in the world, the purpose of which is still largely only guessed at. This imposing archaeological site is often ascribed mystical or spiritual associations and receives thousands of visitors from all over the world each year.

THE CHANNEL ISLANDS

Britains' southernmost islands lie some 14 miles off the French coast, yet despite many French place names, they have not been owned by France since William the Conqueror. Each has its own appeal and the islanders, proud of their heritage, will afford the warmest of welcomes.

GUERNSEY

With a modern airport, excellent harbour, a wide range of attractive accommodation and many unique attractions, Guernsey is a haven for the holiday maker. St Peter Port, the capital, is a busy commercial centre and harbour. The Little Chapel is the smallest in the world, lavishly decorated and with room for only five worshippers at a time. Victor Hugo lived in exile in the town for 15 years and his former home, Hauteville House, is now a museum. There are a host of other museums, a butterfly centre and a variety of archeological sites as well as spectacular cliff walks and beautiful countryside to explore.

JERSEY

Jersey is the largest and most southerly of the Channel Islands and measures just 45 square miles. Leave the car behind and make tracks on foot or pedal along green country lanes. Discover the island's fascinating history - in just a short distance, it is possible to travel from prehistoric to postwar times. In the east, the 13th century Mont Orgueil Castle overlooks Grouville Bay. The Maritime Museum celebrates Jersey's long association with the sea, while the Jersey War Tunnels record the occupation of Jersey during the second world war. The Durrell Wildlife Conservation Trust is a 'must see' for any visitor to the island.

ALDERNEY, HERM & SARK

Alderney is just 1.5 miles wide and 3.5 miles long and is known as 'the most English' of the islands. It has an abundance of flora, fauna and wildlife, beautiful beaches and a relaxed friendly lifestyle. Sights include St Anne's Church, often referred to as The Cathedral of the Channel Islands, the Alderney Society Museum, covering the island's history and development, the lighthouse and Alderney Railway, the only one in the Islands, dubbed The Orient Express and a favourite for railway enthusiasts and children alike. There are boat services to unspoilt Herm, which measures just half a mile square and can be covered on foot in a couple of hours, and to Sark, the smallest of the main Channel islands, which boasts 40 miles of picturesque coastline and no cars - travel is by bicycle or horsedrawn cart. The beautiful walled gardens of Sark's Seigneurie are one of the most popular attractions and the island was designated a Dark-Sky community in 2011, being the first Dark-Sky island in the world, sufficiently clear of light pollution to allow naked-eye astronomy.

HUDSON'S HISTORIC HOUSES & GARDENS HIGHLIGHTS

Athelhampton House and Gardens
(01305) 848363
www.athelhampton.co.uk
One of the finest 15th century Houses in England nestled in the heart of the picturesque Piddle Valley in the famous Hardy county of rural Dorset.

Chavenage
(01666) 502329
www.chavenage.com
Elizabethan Manor Chavenage House, a TV/Film location is still a family home, offers unique experiences, with history, ghosts and more.

Clovelly Village
(01237) 431781
www.clovelly.co.uk
Most visitors consider Clovelly to be unique. Whatever your view, it is a world of difference not to be missed.

Hartland Abbey & Gardens
(01237) 441496/234
www.hartlandabbey.com
Hartland Abbey is a family home full of history in a beautiful valley leading to a wild Atlantic cove.

Sausmarez Manor
(01481) 235571
www.sausmarezmanor.co.uk
A delightful manor to tour, crammed with the history of the family since C1220. Fine example of Queen Anne Colonial architecture.

St Michael's Mount
(01736) 710507
www.stmichaelsmount.co.uk
Explore the amazing island of St Michael's Mount and discover legend, myth and over a thousand years of incredible history.

Sudeley Castle
(01242) 604244
www.sudeleycastle.co.uk
The former home of Tudor Queen, Katharine Parr. Fascinating exhibitons and award-winning gardens. A must-see on any visit to the Cotswolds.

Tintagel Castle - English Heritage
(01840) 770328
www.english-heritage.org.uk/tintagel
Tintagel Castle is a magical day with its wonderful location, set high on the rugged north Cornwall coast.

Wilton House
(01722) 746714
www.wiltonhouse.com
Wilton House has one of the finest art collections in Europe and is set in magnificent landscaped parkland featuring the Palladian Bridge.

HUDSON'S HISTORIC HOUSES & GARDENS
MUSEUMS & HERITAGE SITES

For more suggestions of great historic days out across Britain visit
www.hudsonsheritage.com

SOUTH WEST
WHERE TO STAY

Entries appear alphabetically by town name in each county.
A key to symbols appears on page 4.

BUDOCK VEAN HOTEL ON THE RIVER

Helford Passage, Mawnan Smith, Falmouth, Cornwall TR11 5LG
T: (01326) 250288 **F:** (01326) 250892
E: relax@budockvean.co.uk **W:** www.budockvean.co.uk

This privately owned, family-run, luxury 4 star hotel really does have it all! Budock Vean is an ideal base when visiting Cornwall. The 65 acres of gardens incorporate woodland, parkland, formal and informal areas, valley garden, pond and a natural foreshore to the Helford River. Trebah and Glendurgan Gardens are within walking distance. Guests can also enjoy unlimited use of the well designed on-site 9 hole golf course, at no extra charge.
Leisure facilities include a spectacular indoor pool, sauna, health spa, outdoor hot tub, tennis courts and snooker. Head Chef Darren Kelly and his team focus on creating menus with Cornish sourced seafood, meats and vegetables. An award winning combination where service, presentation and atmosphere are first class. From the jetty, a ferry can take you to a riverside pub or enjoy a private charter on the "Hannah-Molly" - splendid and unique - this is Budock Vean.

DINING: 4 course table d'hôte dinner £40; À la carte, lunch & special diets available; last orders 2100; breakfast from 0800.

BEDROOMS: 57
All bedrooms are well presented with every comfort and facility provided. A few select luxury self-catering cottages are also on site.

B&B PER ROOM PER NIGHT:
S: £73.00 - £141.00
D: £146.00 - £282.00

ADDITIONAL INFORMATION:
Open all year except 2-24 January.

Pets welcome £8.00 per night.

Site: ✿ **P Payment:** 💳 € **Leisure:** ▶ ♨ ⚔ ♟ ⚲ ≋ ⚲ **Property:** ⚑ 🐾 ▭ ▣ ⚒ ◐ **Children:** 🐴 ▥ 🎎
Catering: (✕ ⚲ 🍽 **Room:** ⚲ ⚲ ☎ ⊡ TV DVD 🖨

HANNAFORE POINT HOTEL

BEDROOMS: 37
The Hannafore hotel in Looe has 37 en suite bedrooms of which most have sea views and some balconies. All bedrooms have tea & coffee making facilities, colour TV, hairdryer and trouser press.

B&B PER ROOM PER NIGHT:
S: £58.00 - £76.00
D: £116.00 - £152.00

ADDITIONAL INFORMATION:
Open all year.

Marine Drive, West Looe, Cornwall PL13 2DG
T: (01503) 263273 **F:** (01503) 263272
E: stay@hannaforepointhotel.com **W:** www.hannaforepointhotel.com

With panoramic views of sea, cliffs and St George's Island, Hannafore Point is conveniently placed for sandy beaches, the town of Looe, and, naturally the facilities for deep sea fishing for which the area is famous. Hannafore Point is an excellent venue for a family holiday. Golf can be booked at discounted rates at St Enodoc, Lanhydrock and Looe courses. Hannafore is on the southwest coastal path and there are several gardens nearby including the Lost Gardens of Heligan, the Eden Project and Cotehele. In addition the famous Looe to Polperro walk starts just outside the hotel. Massage and hydrotherapy available by appointment. Headland Restaurant offers table d'hôte and à la carte menus, using fresh, local ingredients including fish bought daily from the fish market. Guests can relax and enjoy the views from Raffles Lounge Bar or the more lively Island Bar on the ground floor.

DINING: 4 course table d'hôte dinner £28; lunch and bar grill available.

AA
★★★
Hotel

Site: P Payment: ▣ **Leisure:** ♪ ▶ ✕ ⚔ 🐟 🎣 **Property:** ⚓ 🐕 ⛪ **Children:** 🛝 🎠 🧸
Catering: (✕ ⚊ 🍽 **Room:** 🛎 ☎ 📺

BERRY HEAD HOTEL

Berry Head, Brixham TQ5 9AJ
T: (01803) 853225 **F:** (01803) 882084
E: stay@berryheadhotel.com **W:** www.berryheadhotel.com

The Berry Head Hotel is set in a superb water's edge position in six acres of its own gardens and woodland, in the seclusion of the Berry Head Country Park, which is noted for its bird life and rare wild flowers. The hotel is steeped in history. It was built as a military hospital in the Napoleonic Wars and was later the home of the Reverend Francis Lyte, who wrote the famous hymn Abide with Me at the hotel, no doubt inspired by the glorious sunsets. The historic fishing port of Brixham, where William of Orange first landed to claim the English crown, is only a short walk away. The comfortable lounge and the restaurant, which overlooks the terrace, enjoy spectacular views of Torbay and the Devon coast.
The emphasis here is upon good food, wine and company in a rather special setting.

DINING: Last orders 2130; bar meals til 2130; special diets available.

BEDROOMS: 32
The hotel offers relaxing accommodation and all rooms have up to date facilities as well as a baby listening service.

B&B PER ROOM PER NIGHT:
S: £58.00 - £76.00
D: £116.00 - £152.00

ADDITIONAL INFORMATION:
Two nights, dinner, b&b from £99 pp/3 nights from £145. Room & breakfast from £50 pp; dinner, room & breakfast from £65 pppn. Boules, squash, sailing, boating, shooting, fishing and birdwatching.

Open all year.

Site: ✿ P **Payment:** ▦ **Leisure:** ♿ ♪ ∪ ✗ ⋈ ⚲ ✎ **Property:** ⚑ ♞ ▦ ⌂ ◗ **Children:** ⚲ ▥
Catering: ⟨✗ ⬚ ⬚ **Room:** ⬚ ⬚ ☎ ⊡

THE DART MARINA HOTEL

BEDROOMS: 49
Elegant, luxury hotel rooms with crisp white linen, deep, fluffy towels and bathrobes and amazing beds which offer rejuvenating sleep of the kind only experienced when breathing in fresh sea air!

B&B PER ROOM PER NIGHT:
S: £115.00 - £155.00
D: £170.00 - £370.00

ADDITIONAL INFORMATION:
Stay five nights on the hotel's dinner, bed & breakfast tariff and only pay for four.

Sandquay Road, Dartmouth, Devon TQ6 9PH
T: (01803) 832580 **F:** (01803) 835040
E: reservations@dartmarina.com **W:** www.dartmarina.com

Dart Marina Hotel, Dartmouth, is a luxury Devon hotel situated on the banks of the River Dart, providing stylish hotel accommodation and self-catering luxury apartments with stunning views over the river. Everything you would expect in a luxury hotel – you'll find in the bedrooms, all with a river view. The health spa eases away the stresses and strains of everyday life with a range of luxury health spa treatments, aromatherapy products and holistic health spa therapies. With panoramic views of breath-taking scenery from every window, Dart Marina's River Restaurant is a fine dining restaurant which holds an AA Rosette in recognition of its high standards of cuisine and a Strawberry icon which illustrates the hotel's commitment to using regional food. Menus combine the very best in seasonal ingredients with the light touch of an exceptional chef, and the atmosphere matches the rest of the hotel – relaxed, chic, understated elegance.

DINING: 3 course table d'hôte dinner £45; à la carte, lunch & special diets available; last orders 2100; breakfast from 0730.

Site: ✿ P **Payment:** 💳 **Leisure:** 🎵 ▶ ♨ ✗ 🍴 ⚘ **Property:** 🐾 🖼 ◐ **Children:** 🛏 🎮 🚶
Catering: (✗ ⟟ 🍽 **Room:** 🛏 💧 ☎ 📺

PLANTATION HOUSE HOTEL & RESTAURANT

Totnes Road, Ermington, Ivybridge, Devon PL21 9NS
T: (01548) 831100
E: info@plantationhousehotel.co.uk **W:** www.plantationhousehotel.co.uk

Formerly the parish rectory, this much loved restaurant with rooms now offers a harmonious blend of relaxed country tranquility and stylish sophistication, with a personal touch. A gently indulgent sanctuary on the very doorstep of river estuaries, soothing beaches, market towns and the wilderness of Dartmoor. Nestling on the green sunny bank of the river Erme valley, in an Area of Outstanding Natural Beauty, Plantation House provides understated comfort in the hands of a loyal, caring team. The kitchen boasts an experienced line up. John the expert fisherman and forager; Richard your chef/patron. Expect fine, locally sourced land and sea ingredients prepared and cooked with great care and expertise. Vegetables, fruits and eggs from the garden; breads, pastries and puddings from the kitchen; and there's a cracking wine list. Breakfasts are irresistible and as indulgent as you may wish. Modern bathrooms are stone clad with under floor heating, bathrobes and classy toiletries.

DINING: Dinner is £39. AA 5* restaurant with rooms. Lighter meals available.

BEDROOMS: 8
Six doubles, one suite, one single.

B&B PER ROOM PER NIGHT:
S: £75.00 - £110.00
D: £120.00 - £230.00

ADDITIONAL INFORMATION:
Open all year.

Site: ❀ P Payment: 💷 Leisure: 🎣 ⚲ ✂ Property: 🖼 ⛵ Children: 🧸 Catering: 🍴 🍷
Room: 🕾 ✆ 📺 📀

THE COTTAGE

BEDROOMS: 31

Dinner, room & breakfast from £53–£102pppn subject to season and room type. 31 en suite bedrooms. The Cottage Hotel is open all year except Jan 2nd - Feb 6th inc.

B&B PER ROOM PER NIGHT:
S: £38.00 - £102.00
D: £76.00 - £174.00

ADDITIONAL INFORMATION:
1st Nov 2015- 26th March 2016 inc, 2 Night stay £56.00-£72.00, 7 Night Stay £53.00-£69.00 according to room. Prices pppn includes 5-course dinner + coffee, room & breakfast. Wi-Fi currently in lounges only.

Hope Cove, Salcombe, Devon TQ7 3HJ
T: (01548) 561555 **F:** (01548) 561455
E: info@hopecove.com **W:** www.hopecove.com

Hope Cove is what the name implies: a beautiful village situated along the rugged South Devon coastline. The Cottage Hotel enjoys a superb position, overlooking the picturesque harbour and cove, set in two and a half acres of shrubs and lawns which lead, via sloping footpaths, to the largest of two beaches, where you can bathe in safety. The Ireland family have run The Cottage since 1973 and provide a warm, personal service, whilst constantly updating the facilities. The Restaurant is renowned amongst visitors and locals alike. Locally caught crab, lobster and fish are on the menu and the house wines are truly special. The Cottage is popular with families - there is a games room and special high teas are available. Along this Heritage Coastline there are challenging walks affording superb views. The area is famous for its unique flora and fauna, including the Nature Reserve at Slapton Ley. Many sporting activities are available nearby with ten golf courses within easy reach - the hotel having concessions at Bigbury, Thurlestone and Dartmouth. New for 2015 season refurbished bar and open-plan lounge with sea-views and local maritime history.

DINING: Bar meals 1200–1400; last orders 2030.
Site: ❋ **Payment:** 💳 **Leisure:** ⚑ **Property:** ⚓ 🐕 🛏 ♨ **Children:** 🐎 🛏 ⚘ **Catering:** ❮❯ ♟ 🍴
Room: 🗞 ⚘ ☎ 📺

AA ★★★★ Guest Accommodation

THE QUEENS ARMS

Corton Denham Road, Corton Denham, Sherbourne DT9 4LR
T: (01963) 220317
E: relax@thequeensarms.com **W:** www.thequeensarms.com

The Queens Arms is situated at the heart of the ancient village of Corton Denham, nestling on the Somerset / Dorset border just north of Sherborne. Surrounded by stunning countryside, this late 18th Century British pub with rooms will delight those in search of good drink, good food and real comfort. Awarded two AA Rosettes for its culinary excellence, finalists in the South West Tourism Pub and B&B/Accommodation of the year 2014/5, Taste of Somerset Best Pub 2013, CAMRA 2012 Cider Pub of the Year and National Best Freehouse for 2012 Awards, makes this a destination pub. Their eight en suite letting rooms have received AA 5 star, why not pay them a visit and see what other people are talking about. As the journalist from The Telegraph wrote 'the Queens Arms, where Chelsea meets the country'.

DINING: Breakfast 0800 - 1000 daily, available to non residents as well. Lunch from £6.50. Dinner, 3 courses £25 - £30. Open for lunch 1200 - 1500 and dinner 1800 - 2200 Monday - Friday and 1800 - 2100 on Sunday.

BEDROOMS: 8
Rooms are individually designed and offers guests a double or twin room with en suite shower or bath with shower facilities, complimentary water, 100% Egyptian cotton linen, goose down duvets, fluffy towels, flat screen TV's with fitted DVD players and tea and coffee facilities.

B&B PER ROOM PER NIGHT:
S: £85.00 - £90.00
D: £110.00 - £130.00

ADDITIONAL INFORMATION:
Open all year.

Site: ❋ P **Payment:** 💷 **Leisure:** ▶ ♻ **Property:** 🐕 🐎 🖼 ♨ **Children:** 🐾 🛏 **Catering:** ⟨✗ 🍴
Room: 📶 🛁 📞 📻 📺 📀 🔌 🖨

PLUMBER MANOR

BEDROOMS: 16
There are six elegant bedrooms within the main house and a further ten in the courtyard and converted barn.

B&B PER ROOM PER NIGHT:
S: £120.00 - £145.00
D: £160.00 - £240.00

ADDITIONAL INFORMATION:
Nov–March 10% discount for 2 nights/15% discount. 3 nights+ exc. Xmas/New Year/Easter. Well located for visiting Sherborne, Shaftesbury, Blandford Forum, Dorchester, Beaminster, Cerne Abbas Lulworth, Studland and the Jurassic Coast.

Sturminster Newton, Dorset DT10 2AF
T: (01258) 472507 **F:** (01258) 473370
E: book@plumbermanor.com **W:** www.plumbermanor.co.uk

This imposing Jacobean manor house is set in idyllic countryside "far from the madding crowd". The Divelish stream weaves its way through delightful grounds, extensive lawns and fine old trees. Dating from the 17th century, the manor has been the home of the Prideaux-Brune family. Since 1973 the careful management of Richard, Alison and Brian (in the kitchen) has led to the creation of a first class hotel and restaurant. Richard knows many of his regular diners personally and is always on hand for advice about dishes on the ever changing menu, and about what to see in this charming part of Dorset. When we dined there we had the excellent seafood trio to start, followed by some very tasty venison. Remember to leave room for one of the famous Plumber puddings, which come round on a trolley! The wine list is of the same standard, well-chosen and with ever changing freshness. Plumber is welcoming, comfortable and has a charming atmosphere in which to relax and savour first class hospitality, cuisine and service. It is a quintessential English country house hotel.

DINING: 2 course table d'hôte dinner From £30 /3 course £38. À la carte, lunch & special diets available; last orders 2130.

Payment: ▣ **Property:** ♟ ♞ **Catering:** ◖✕ ♟

THE INN AT FOSSEBRIDGE

Fossebridge, Near Cheltenham, Gloucestershire GL54 3JS
T: (01285) 720721
E: info@fossebridgeinn.co.uk W: www.fossebridgeinn.co.uk

There has been an Inn at Fossebridge located on the banks of the River Coln, between Northleach and Cirencester, for more than 300 years. Experienced hotelier Dee Ludlow and her partner Geoff Collins have become the new owners and are busy enhancing this beautiful building and introducing an exceptional casual dining concept within the character Cotswold pub with stone walls and flagstone floors and beams. There are two magnificent dining/meeting rooms which seat up to 60 for banqueting/weddings and the beautiful Georgian windows overlook four acres of stunning gardens and the lake - absolutely perfect for Al Fresco dining. In the grounds are two charming holiday cottages, renovated to a very high standard. Lakeside House sleeps 10 and Stable Cottage sleeps four adults and two children. The Inn is located on the Fosse Way, in the centre of the Cotswolds and its many famous attractions. It is a popular wedding venue both for the ceremony and the reception.

DINING: Restaurant open all day from 1200 - 2100 (last orders). Average price £28.00 for three course food only.

BEDROOMS: 9
There are nine luxurious bedrooms in the main house including Principal, Superior and Classic rooms and each is named after a nearby Cotswold town – for example Burford, Tetbury and Moreton in Marsh. Each one is different and furnished with antique and period furniture.

B&B PER ROOM PER NIGHT:
S: £75.00 - £125.00
D: £100.00 - £150.00

ADDITIONAL INFORMATION:
Open all year.

Site: ✿ **P Payment:** ▣ **Leisure:** ▶ ♺ ⚲ **Property:** ♟ ♞ ▣ ⛪ **Children:** ⛹ ▥ ✦ **Catering:** (✕ ▼ ▦
Room: ▨ ♨ ☎ ▣

THE WHITE HART ROYAL

BEDROOMS: 28

Bedrooms are some of the best in the area, with a number of ground floor garden rooms accessible via the courtyard. They are divided into singles, twins, doubles and feature bedrooms, like, the King Charles Suite and the Four-Poster Rooms. The Le Noir Room has a double bathtub.

B&B PER ROOM PER NIGHT:
S: £75.00 - £95.00
D: £95.00 - £135.00

ADDITIONAL INFORMATION:
With a civil wedding licence this is the ideal place for a wedding or naming ceremony.

High Street, Moreton in Marsh, Gloucestershire GL56 0BA
T: (01608) 650731 **F:** (01608) 650880
E: whr@bulldogmail.co.uk **W:** www.whitehartroyal.co.uk

The White Hart Royal stands in the centre of this busy Cotswold market town. Built as a coaching inn in the 17th century and put on the map by King Charles I who stayed here on the eve of the battle of Marston Moor nearby. The property has been cleverly refurbished whilst maintaining its period features. The popular Courtyard Restaurant has been awarded an AA Rosette for cuisine. You can eat al fresco or enjoy the relaxed atmosphere of the Snug Bar with its inglenook fireplace. Cuisine is contemporary English using local produce where possible, accompanied by a good selection of old and new world wines. Moreton-in-Marsh is blessed with good shops, a famous market and the Batsford Arboretum. Hidcote, Kiftsgate and Snowshill Gardens, and the rolling north Cotswolds are nearby.

DINING: Courtyard Restaurant à la carte starters from £5, mains from £10, desserts from £5.

Site: ✿ P **Payment:** 🖃 **Leisure:** ∪ **Property:** 🍴 🐕 🛏 ⛪ ◐ **Children:** 🐾 🛏 🏃 **Catering:** ⟨✗ 🍴 🍽 **Room:** 🔌 🚿 📞 📺 📀 💇 🧺

THE LORDLEAZE HOTEL

Henderson Drive, Forton Road, Chard, Somerset TA20 2HW
T: (01460) 61066 **F:** (01460) 66468
E: info@lordleazehotel.com **W:** www.lordleazehotel.com

The Lordleaze Hotel, once an 18th century farmhouse offers cosiness and unfussy conviviality coupled with contemporary efficiency. Tea can be taken on the terrace overlooking a well-tended garden and the natural pasture land beyond. The Owen family ensure that guests are warmly welcomed: fed with generosity and flair from locally sourced products, especially fresh fish delivered daily and the local farms which supply us with quality meat, all freshly cooked and served in the conservatory and garden room restaurants. Lordleaze is a peaceful, friendly and comfortable hotel conveniently located at the convergence of the counties of Dorset, Somerset and Devon. Bristol, Exeter, Taunton and Yeovil are within a comfortable drive, as is Lyme Regis and the Jurassic Coast line. There are many historic houses and gardens to visit in the area. But don't miss Chard's own museum with its display of John Stringfellow's first powered airplane.

DINING: 3 course à la carte from £27.50, special diets catered for, last orders 2115, breakfast from 0715 weekdays, 0815 weekends.

Site: ❋ **P Payment:** 💳 **Property:** 🍴 🐾 📻 📺 **Children:** 🍼 🛏 🔥 **Catering:** 🍴 🍷 🍴
Room: ☕ 🚿 📞 📺 🎧 🚪

BEDROOMS: 25
25 en suite bedrooms, all bedrooms being double or twin bedded and available for single occupancy. There are ground floor bedrooms, a room with disabled facilities, family rooms, and a 4 poster bedroom.

B&B PER ROOM PER NIGHT:
S: £79.00 - £82.00
D: £125.00 - £135.00

ADDITIONAL INFORMATION:
Open all year.

AA
★★★
Hotel

THE PEAR TREE AT PURTON

BEDROOMS: 17
Bedrooms are divided into Executive, with spa baths, and Standard or Vicarage. All are furnished to a high standard and offer a host of luxury amenities.

B&B PER ROOM PER NIGHT:
S: £104.00 - £119.00
D: £109.00 - £149.00

ADDITIONAL INFORMATION:
Open all year. (Closed 25 & 26 Dec). The hotel is just five miles from the M4 and Swindon, with its Railway Museum and Designer Shopping Outlet. The South Cotswolds, Longleat, Bath, Blenheim and Stonehenge are all nearby.

Church End, Purton, Swindon, Wiltshire SN5 4ED
T: (01793) 772100 **F:** (01793) 772369
E: stay@peartreepurton.co.uk **W:** www.peartreepurton.co.uk

Originally the Saxon village vicarage, this Cotswold stone hotel is set in seven acres on the outskirts of Purton village between the Cotswolds and the Marlborough Downs. The Vicarage has been extended and between the two halves is a spectacular galleried hall and landing. Dedication to good service has made this a very successful hotel. Proprietor Anne Young has now been joined by daughter Alix and son-in-law Tim. They and their staff succeed in putting guests immediately at ease. Stylish function rooms make the Pear Tree a venue suitable for many occasions. Dining is in the spacious AA two Rosette Conservatory Restaurant, overlooking the gardens with their giant chess set, herbaceous borders, wild flower meadow, wetlands and own vineyard, which produces the praised English wine Cuvee Alix. The restaurant specialises in modern English cuisine using the freshest local ingredients.

DINING: One course lunch from £10 with main meals on the à la carte menu starting at £16. Open 7 days a week for lunch & dinner.

Site: ❀ P **Payment:** 💳 € **Leisure:** 🏊 ▶ ⛳ **Property:** 🎣 🐾 🖥 ♨ **Children:** 🧸 ⚲
Catering: (✗ 🍽 🍴 **Room:** 🛎 🌡 ☎ 📺 📀 🔌

THE MOORINGS HOTEL

The Moorings Hotel, Gorey Pier, St Martin, Jersey JE3 6EW
T: (01534) 853633
E: reservations@themooringshotel.com **W:** www.themooringshotel.com

The Moorings Hotel and Restaurant enjoys a true Jersey "picture postcard" location. Situated below the historic ramparts of Mont Orgueil Castle, on the waterfront of Gorey Harbour. The Moorings Restaurant has two AA Rosettes and is one of the island's finest. Simon truly excels in the kitchen! Both the table d'hôte and à la carte menus offer a wonderful selection of island produce with an accent on local seafood. Presentation, menu choices and service are all exemplary - this restaurant justly deserves its long standing highly regarded reputation. Joanne takes control of all front of house activities, with the kitchen in the hands of her husband/chef Simon Walker. You could not wish for a better team to run this lovely hotel where such friendly hospitality is extended. The Pier Bar and Bistro offers a more casual dining experience overlooking Gorey Harbour, where you can savour local fish specialities. The al fresco terrace is the place to absorb the warmth of this delightful hotel and soak up the rays of an amazing sunset. This is a great location and The Moorings must be enjoyed on any visit to the beautiful island of Jersey. Highly recommended in all respects.

DINING: Walkers Restaurant à la carte. Lunch & special diets available.

Payment: 💳 **Property:** 🐾 📺 ♨ ∅ **Children:** 🧒 **Catering:** ⟨✗ 🍴 **Room:** 🔌 ☎ 💻 📺

BEDROOMS: 15
All bedrooms have all the modern amenities, including satellite television, radio, trouser press, hair dryer, tea and coffee making facilities, direct dial telephone and modem points. Rooms are very well presented and have all facilities expected for the comfort of today's travellers. Many enjoy stunning sea views towards Grouville Bay across the harbour.

B&B PER ROOM PER NIGHT:
S: £57.50 - £77.50
D: £139.00 - £162.00

ADDITIONAL INFORMATION:
Open all year.

AA
★★★
Hotel

Oxfordshire
Buckinghamshire
Berkshire
Surrey   Kent
Hampshire
Sussex
Isle of Wight

SOUTH EAST

Berkshire, Buckinghamshire, Hampshire, Isle of Wight, Kent, Oxfordshire, Surrey, Sussex

The Thames sweeps eastwards in broad graceful curves, cutting through the beeches of the Chiltern Hills. Miles of glorious countryside and historic cities offer heritage sites, gardens, parks and impressive architecture for you to visit. In the far south, fun-filled resorts and interesting harbours are dotted along 257 miles of delightful coastline and the Isle of Wight is a only a short ferry ride away. The South East of England is an area of great beauty that will entice you to return again and again.

SOUTH EAST

BERKSHIRE

Renowned for its royal connections, the romantic county of Berkshire counts Windsor Castle as its most famous building. Cliveden House, former seat of the Astor family and now a famous hotel, is nearby. Highclere Castle, the setting for Downton Abbey, as well as Eton College and Ascot Racecourse can be found here too.

BUCKINGHAMSHIRE

Buckinghamshire, to the north east of the region, is home to the most National Trust properties in the country as well as the magnificent 'Capability Brown' landscape at Stowe, now a famous public school.

The city of Milton Keynes has its infamous concrete cows and the delights of its vast shopping centre but there's plenty more to see and do in the county. Experience a hands-on history lesson at the fascinating Chiltern Open Air Museum or for a gentler pace, enjoy a tranquil bike ride through beautiful countryside along the meandering Thames.

Windsor Castle
Windsor, Berkshire SL4 1NJ
(020) 7766 7304
www.royalcollection.org.uk
Built by Edward III in the 14th century and restored by later monarchs, Windsor Castle is the largest and oldest occupied castle in the world. It is an official residence of Her Majesty the Queen and encapsulates more than 900 years of English history.

HAMPSHIRE & ISLE OF WIGHT

Historic Winchester is a must-visit for its charming medieval streets, imposing Cathedral, vibrant galleries and stylish, independent shops. The ancient heaths and woodlands of the New Forest National Park were once a royal hunting ground for William the Conqueror and deer, ponies and cattle continue to roam free. Cycle, walk or go horseriding in this tranquil, car-free environment or visit attractions such as the National Motor Museum at Beaulieu and Exbury Gardens & Steam Railway for a great day out.

Coastal Hampshire, with the Solent, Southampton Water and the Isle of Wight, is one of the sailing playgrounds of England. Nearby Portsmouth Harbour has Nelson's Victory, the Mary Rose and the ironclad HMS Warrior. Stroll gently around the picturesque village of Lymington or explore the cliffs along the coast. The Isle of Wight can be reached by ferry and is a great destination for amazing beaches, exciting events, or a step back in time, counting Osborne House and Carisbrooke Castle among its historic gems.

Osborne House
East Cowes, Isle of Wight PO32 6JX
(01983) 200022
www.english-heritage.org.uk
Step into Queen Victoria's favourite country home and experience a world unchanged since the country's longest reigning monarch died here just over 100 years ago.

KENT

The Garden of England is a diverse county full of romantic villages and unmissable heritage. The opulent Leeds Castle, surrounded by its shimmering lake and set in 500 acres of spectacular parkland and gardens, has attractions and events aplenty. Take a tour of Kent's rural past with a scenic cruise along the River Medway to Kent Life, a museum and working farm with animals galore and a real sense of nostalgia for bygone days. At the northeast tip of the county, where stunning sea- and sky-scapes famously inspired JMW Turner, Margate is home to the brilliant Turner Contemporary art gallery and the Shell Grotto, a subterranean wonder lined with 4.6 million shells. Broadstairs hosts an acclaimed annual folk festival and Ramsgate is a firm favourite, with its sophisticated café culture, marina and award-winning sandy beach.

OXFORDSHIRE

Oxford's dreaming spires, echoing quads and cloistered college lawns have a timeless beauty. The Ashmolean Museum, Britain's oldest public museum, opened in 1683 and contains gold and jewellery believed to have belonged to King Alfred, the lantern carried by Guy Fawkes and riches from ancient Egypt and Greece. The Bodleian Library, founded in 1596, contains over one million volumes, including a copy of every book published in the UK since 1900. Just north of Oxford at Woodstock sits magnificent Blenheim Palace. Oxfordshire's quiet paths and roads are perfect for cycling, and charming picture postcard villages like Great Tew make excellent rest points.

Blenheim Palace
Woodstock, Oxfordshire OX20 1PX
(0800) 849 6500
www.blenheimpalace.com
Birthplace of Sir Winston Churchill and seat of the Duke of Marlborough, Blenheim Palace, one of the finest baroque houses in England, is set in over 2,000 acres of landscaped gardens.

SURREY

Ashdown Forest, now more of a heath, covers 6400 acres of upland, with a large deer, badger and rare bird population. The heights of Box Hill and Leith Hill rise above the North Downs to overlook large tracts of richly wooded countryside, containing a string of well protected villages. The Devil's Punchbowl, near Hindhead, is a two mile long sandstone valley, overlooked by the 900-ft Gibbet Hill. Farnham, in the west of the country, has Tudor and Georgian houses flanking the 12th century castle. Nearby Aldershot is the home of the British Army and county town Guildford is a contemporary business and shopping centre with a modern cathedral and university. The north of the county borders Greater London and includes the 2400 acre Richmond Park, Hampton Court Palace and Kew Gardens.

SUSSEX

Sussex is a popular county for those wanting a short break from the hustle and bustle of London. Cosmopolitan Brighton, surely the capital of East Sussex, oozes culture, boutique hotels, marina, shops and 'buzz'. The eccentric Royal Pavilion testifies to its history as the Regency summer capital of Britain.

Pashley Manor Gardens
Wadhurst, East Sussex TN5 7HE
(01580) 200888
www.pashleymanorgardens.com
Pashley Manor Gardens offer a blend of romantic landscaping, imaginative plantings, fine old trees, fountains, springs and large ponds plus exciting special events.

To the west is the impressive Arundel Castle, with its famous drama festival, nearby popular marinas and Wittering sands. Bognor Regis is a traditional seaside resort with a blue flag beach and the usual attractions. To the east the impressive Beachy Head and Seven Sisters cliffs provide a dramatic backdrop for Eastbourne. The Sussex section of the South Downs National Park stretches from Beachy Head to Harting Down with miles of open chalk grassland, lush river valleys and ancient forests to explore.

If heritage is your thing then Sussex has a plethora of historic houses and gardens and three of the historic cinque ports. Rye in particular, with its cobbled streets, transports the visitor back three centuries. The 1066 Story is told at Battle, near Hastings and Groombridge Place, Great Dixter and Borde Hill all feature stunningly beautiful heritage gardens.

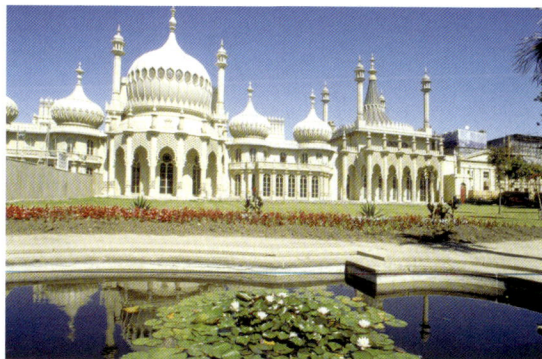

HUDSON'S HISTORIC HOUSES & GARDENS HIGHLIGHTS

Arundel Castle & Gardens
(01903) 882173
www.arundelcastle.org
Ancient Castle, Stately Home, Gardens & the Collector Earl's Garden.

Beaulieu Estate
(01590) 612345
www.beaulieu.co.uk
Beaulieu, at the heart of the New Forest, is home to Lord Montagu and features a range of heritage attractions.

Blenheim Palace
(0800) 8496500
www.blenheimpalace.com
Blenheim Palace is seat of the 11th Duke and Duchess of Marlborough and the birthplace of Sir Winston Churchill.

Broughton Castle
(01295) 276070
www.broughtoncastle.com
"*About the most beautiful castle in all England.... For sheer loveliness of the combination of water, woods and picturesque buildings.*" Sir Charles Oman (1898).

Chenies Manor House
(01494) 762888
www.cheniesmanorhouse.co.uk
The manor house is in the picturesque village of Chenies and lies in the beautiful Chiltern Hills.

Goodwood House
(01243) 755012
www.goodwood.com
Goodwood House, ancestral home of the Dukes of Richmond and Gordon with magnificent art collection.

Great Dixter Garden
(01797) 252878
www.greatdixter.co.uk
A very special garden with a great deal of character, planted with flair, always something to see, whatever the season.

Hever Castle & Gardens
(01732) 865224
www.hevercastle.co.uk
Experience 700 years of colourful history and spectacular award-wining gardens at the childhood home of Anne Boleyn.

Lancing College Chapel
(01273) 465949
www.lancingcollege.co.uk
"*I know of no more spectacular post - Reformation ecclesiastical building in the kingdom.*" Evelyn Waugh, former pupil.

Penshurst Place and Gardens
(01892) 870307
www.penshurstplace.com
One of Engalnd's greatest family-owned historic houses with a history spanning nearly seven centuries.

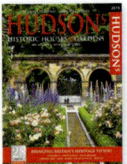

For more suggestions of great historic days out across Britain visit
www.hudsonsheritage.com

SOUTH EAST
WHERE TO STAY

Entries appear alphabetically by town name in each county.

A key to symbols appears on page 4.

CANTLEY HOUSE HOTEL

Milton Road, Wokingham RG40 5QG
T: (0118) 989 5107 **F:** (0118) 989 5105
E: reservations@cantleyhotel.co.uk **W:** www.cantleyhotel.co.uk

Cantley House Hotel was formerly the home of the Marquis of Ormonde. Built in 1880, it was converted into an hotel in 1983. It sits in five acres of garden and parkland just five minutes from Wokingham town centre, ten minutes from the M4, and one hour from Central London, yet is quiet and self-contained. Cantley House is a popular conference and wedding venue, although weddings do not impinge on the privacy of other guests as they take place in the dedicated Pipers Lounge or in the Briar converted barn. It offers very good value to business travellers working in Reading or Bracknell and looking for a hotel with individuality and exceptional service, and also to leisure guests visiting Windsor Castle or Dorney Wood. Wokingham Theatre is next door to the hotel.

DINING: 1 AA Rosette dining in Miltons Restaurant. Table d'hôte 3 course dinner from £28.50; à la carte & special diets available. Last dinner orders 2130; breakfast from 0700.

BEDROOMS: 36
Bedrooms, each individually furnished with antiques, are spacious and comfortable. Superior rooms and suites have Jacuzzi baths. Our favourites were the ten Executive ground floor rooms in The Clocktower Wing, added in 2001, each opening onto a private terrace and garden.

B&B PER ROOM PER NIGHT:
D: £99.00 - £199.00

ADDITIONAL INFORMATION:
Open all year.

Site: ❀ P Payment: 💷 € Leisure: 🎿 🍴 ⚲ Property: 🍷 🐕 📺 🔴 ◐ ⬤ Children: 🛏 🎿
Catering: (✕ 🍷 🍴 Room: 🔌 🚿 📞 📺

MONTAGU ARMS HOTEL

BEDROOMS: 22
Sumptuous rooms and suites are sophisticated and comfortable with attractive décor – the themes being romance and luxury.

B&B PER ROOM PER NIGHT:
S: £154.00 - £308.00
D: £208.00 - £358.00

ADDITIONAL INFORMATION:
Local attractions Beaulieu Abbey & Motor Museum. Exbury Gardens, the New Forest Otter & Wildlife Park and Bucklers Hard Maritime Museum are within easy reach.

Palace Lane, Beaulieu, Brockenhurst SO42 7ZL
T: (01590) 612324 **F:** (01590) 612188
E: reservations@montaguarmshotel.co.uk **W:** www.montaguarmshotel.co.uk

Timeless elegance and unique charm are the hallmarks of this glorious 17th century house, set in a stunning New Forest location. Some rooms have views towards Beaulieu Palace and others look across the picturesque gardens. At the Michelin starred, AA Rosette Terrace Restaurant, menus compiled by head chef and Roux scholar Matthew Tomkinson use the finest quality seasonal ingredients, as far as possible local, free range and organic. Herbs and vegetables in season come from the hotel's own kitchen garden. There is a fine wine list including organic, unoaked and prestigious vintages. Monty's Inn offers a less formal brasserie menu. Afternoon teas, with home made scones, jams and a choice of Fair Trade teas and coffee are very popular. The hotel makes a stunning wedding venue, either on an exclusive use basis or for a smaller intimate ceremony for up to 30 people. Hotel guests can be pampered at the award winning Senspa at nearby sister hotel Carey's Manor. The Montagu Arms is a luxurious base for a visit to this beautiful area at any time of year.

DINING: Michelin starred, AA Rosette Terrace Restaurant and Monty's Inn offers a less formal brasserie menu.
Site: ❀ **P Payment:** 💳 **Leisure:** ♪ ▶ ♨ ✗ **Property:** ⚑ 📺 🖥 ⚙ ◐ ∅ **Children:** ⛷ 🛏 ☂
Catering: ✕ 🍸 **Room:** ☎ 📠

THE WHITE HORSE HOTEL

Market Place, Romsey, Hampshire SO51 8ZJ
T: (01794) 512431 **F:** (01794) 517485
E: thewhitehorse@twhromsey.com **W:** www.thewhitehorseromsey.co.uk

The White Horse, a Grade II listed building, is one of only three late medieval structures in Hampshire that was designed as a purpose built Inn. From the bygone days of the stagecoach, for over 400 years, the White Horse has extended hospitality to guests. This stunning and historic Inn, situated in the heart of the market town of Romsey, is now the principal hotel for visiting this area of Hampshire - gateway to the New Forest and close to cathedral cities and coastal destinations. Standards are superb throughout. The Brasserie is more contemporary in style and serves acclaimed two AA Rosette award-winning cuisine, sourced locally, presented with flair and attentive professionalism. Public areas exude sophisticated style from Tudor influences up to today's eclectic elegance. The White Horse is the perfect base for visiting Hampshire or, for a weekend away just to relax and savour the history, hospitality and charm that this lovely hotel has to offer.

DINING: À la carte, lunch & special diets available; last orders 2200; breakfast from 0700.

BEDROOMS: 31
Rooms are beautifully designed and luxury refinements provided. The Penthouse Suite is sumptuous and the Loft apartments characterful.

B&B PER ROOM PER NIGHT:
S: £90.00 - £105.00
D: £115.00 - £165.00

ADDITIONAL INFORMATION:
In summer months, the picturesque courtyard for dining and socialising is a must! The Tack and Forge Suite is available for up to 40 persons. The recently refurbished Stables is available for up to 80 persons.

Site: ❀ P **Payment:** 💷 **Property:** 🐕 🐎 ♉ ◑ **Children:** 🧺 🛏 ⚹ **Catering:** ⦅✕ 🍷 🍽
Room: 🍵 ♨ 📞 📺 📀

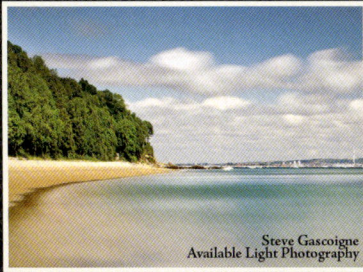

Steve Gascoigne
Available Light Photography

THE PRIORY BAY HOTEL

BEDROOMS: 20
Principal and classic rooms are in the main building, where as the converted Tithe Barns are more suitable for families. £300-£375 based on four sharing. Self-catering accommodation is also available.

B&B PER ROOM PER NIGHT:
S: £90.00 - £225.00
D: £160.00 - £300.00

ADDITIONAL INFORMATION:
The hotel is available for weddings and has a wedding pavilion on the beach. For an extra treat, guests can choose from a range of holistic therapy treatments in the comfort of their own room.

Priory Drive, Seaview, Isle of Wight PO34 5BU
T: (01983) 613146
E: enquiries@priorybay.co.uk **W:** www.priorybay.co.uk

This elegant Virginia creeper-clad country retreat has been built upon by medieval monks, Tudor farmers and Georgian gentry. The Priory Bay sits atop a small valley overlooking a stunning 70 acre estate, with spectacular views over its own private beach, six hole golf course and the East Solent. Its medley of beautiful buildings have been restored to create the unique "Country House Hotel by the Sea", which has become synonymous with fine dining, service and luxury. Facilities include tennis courts, an outdoor swimming pool (open June-September, weather permitting) and, reputedly, the best-six hole golf course in the South of England. The property has two dining options. The Regency-muralled Island Room and the brasserie-style Priory Oyster Restaurant with al fresco terrace, which offers seasonal cuisine specialising in local and foraged produce. The estate is a haven for wildlife, including birds of prey, owls, red squirrels and orchids. The hotel is available for weddings and also has a wedding pavilion on the beach where couples can get married.

DINING: Table d'hôte dinner £35. Lunch & special diets available; last orders 2115.

Site: ❀ **P Payment:** 💳 **Leisure:** 🎵 ▶ ♄ ⚔ 🎿 ⚲ ⚲ **Property:** 🐕 🐎 🚂 🛏 ◑ ⊘ **Children:** 🐴 ▥ 🎎
Catering: (✕ 🍷 🍽 **Room:** 🔌 🚿 📞 📺 📀

ROMNEY BAY HOUSE

Coast Road, Littlestone, New Romney, Kent TN28 8QY
T: (01797) 364747 **F:** (01797) 367156
E: romneybayhouse@aol.co.uk **W:** www.romneybayhousehotel.co.uk

Built in the 1920s for the American actress Hedda Hopper and designed by Sir Clough Williams-Ellis of Portmeirion fame, Romney Bay House is owned by Clinton and Lisa Lovell, who are most welcoming hosts. The hotel is situated along a private road on a totally unspoiled stretch of coastline with spectacular sea views. The drawing room overlooks the terrace with the sea beyond and the first floor look-out room has a library and board games. There is a croquet lawn and two golf courses immediately behind the hotel. Clinton cooks a four-course set dinner (different every night) which guests can meander through while watching the last golfers through the window of the conservatory restaurant. The freshest local produce is used and there is a select but fine wine list. Cream teas are also a speciality. The natural wildness of Romney Marsh and the proximity of the rolling Kent countryside and the historic Cinque Ports make this an ideal spot for a few days' relaxation.

DINING: 4 course set dinner £45 served at 2000 Tues, Wed, Fri & Sats; special diets available.

BEDROOMS: 10
The ten bedrooms, including two four-posters, are exceptionally well appointed with cheerful antique furniture.

ADDITIONAL INFORMATION:
Single room including breakfast from £70; double from £95. Winter Breaks Nov–Feb, Tues & Wed winter 2 night break, superior sea view.

Site: ✿ P Payment: 💳 Leisure: ▶ Property: ♟ 🖥 ♒ ⌀ Catering: (✕ ♟ 🍴 Room: 🔌 💧 ☎ 📺 📀

MILL HOUSE HOTEL & RESTAURANT

BEDROOMS: 21
All rooms come with flat screen TV, Wi-Fi throughout, complimentary Duck Island toiletries and a hospitality tray with delicious home made biscuits.

B&B PER ROOM PER NIGHT:
S: £87.50
D: £100.00

ADDITIONAL INFORMATION:
Open all year. Kingham itself was voted England's Favourite Village recently by Country Life Magazine. Oxford, Bicester and Cheltenham are all within 30 minutes drive.

Station Road, Kingham, Oxfordshire OX7 6UH
T: (01608) 658188 **F:** (01608) 658492
E: stay@millhousehotel.co.uk **W:** www.millhousehotel.co.uk

Built in 1770 on the site of an earlier flour mill listed in the Domesday Book, original fireplaces and bread ovens, as well as original flagstone flooring, can still be seen in the public rooms. Built of Cotswold stone, The Mill House, set in ten acres of stunning gardens and with its own trout stream, characterises the beautiful architectural style of the area. The hotel is now owned by local family Paul & Maria Drinkwater, who have revitalized the dining and bar areas already and are upgrading the 21 bedrooms. Most overlook the gardens or rolling Cotswold countryside. Head chef Matt Dare strives, wherever possible, to use local suppliers sourcing the finest organic ingredients in the Mill Brook restaurant. Lighter fare is available in the Mill Bar with a selection of real ales on tap, or in the Cotswold Lounge, open all day. The Mill House makes an excellent base for visiting the surrounding villages and attractions including Birdland and the Model Village at Bourton-on-the-Water, Batsford Arboretum and the antique shops of Stow-on-the-Wold.

DINING: Lunch 1200 – 1400; Monday - Saturday and 1200 -1430 Sunday. Evening meals 1830 -2100 seven days a week. £28.50 for two courses; £32.50 for three courses.

Site: ✿ P **Payment:** 💳 **Property:** 🚬 🐴 🚪 🗄 🍴 **Children:** 🚸 **Catering:** 🍴 🍷 🍽 **Room:** 🍵 ☕ 📞 📺

DEANS PLACE HOTEL

Seaford Road, Alfriston, East Sussex BN26 5TW
T: (01323) 870248 **F:** (01323) 870918
E: mail@deansplacehotel.co.uk **W:** www.deansplacehotel.co.uk

Alfriston is a picture postcard village nestling in the South Downs, with the Cuckmere river running through it, just behind the hotel, antique and curio shops, a 14th century church, a 15th century pub and the Old Clergy House. The South Downs Way runs beside the river and Drusilla's Zoo Park is just outside the village. Originally the centre of a large farming estate, Deans Place became a hotel at the beginning of the 20th century. The hotel offers a full events programme throughout the year with many themed evenings and weekend break offers. Sunday night special, dinner, b&b from £120 per room. Winter Warmer from £119 dinner, b&b per room. Summer 4 Night Break, dinner, B&B £550 per room, per stay.

DINING: 3 course à la carte dinner £38; lunch & special diets available; last orders 2130; breakfast from 0700. 2 Rosette awarded. Dining available outside on the terrace.

BEDROOMS: 36
This family run hotel has 36 individually styled en suite bedrooms, from singles to executives with beautiful views, freeview TV, & DVD player.

B&B PER ROOM PER NIGHT:
S: £37.50 - £97.50
D: £90.00 - £160.00

ADDITIONAL INFORMATION:
Deans Place is handy for Brighton, Lewes, Glyndebourne Opera and the many attractions of the Sussex coast.

AA
★★★
Hotel

Site: ✿ **P** **Payment:** 💷 **Leisure:** ⚓ **Property:** 🍴 🐾 🛏 🎱 ◑ **Children:** 🎠 🏠 ⚲ **Catering:** ⟨X ⚓ 🍴
Room: ♨ ♨ ☏ ⌨ 📺 📀 ⚲ 🚪

POWDERMILLS HOTEL

BEDROOMS: 49
There are 49 individually decorated en suite bedrooms, some with four posters.

B&B PER ROOM PER NIGHT:
S: £100.00 - £125.00
D: £130.00 - £195.00

ADDITIONAL INFORMATION:
Weddings, conferences, meetings and private parties can be catered for by professional and efficient staff in two large function rooms for up to 250 guests.

Powdermill Lane, Battle, East Sussex TN33 0SP
T: (01424) 775511 **F:** (01424) 774540
E: powdc@aol.com **W:** www.powdermillshotel.com

The PowderMills is a stunning privately owned Listed Georgian country house hotel set in 150 acres of parkland, lakes and woods, adjoining the famous 1066 Battlefield and Abbey. Guests can explore beautiful woodland trails and fish for carp and pike in the seven acre lake, or enjoy the outdoor swimming pool in season. The hotel has a relaxed, welcoming atmosphere and exudes period charm with rooms full of comfy sofas, antiques, interesting artwork and a selection of good books. Public rooms have wonderful log fires in winter. The hotel is ideally located for exploring Sussex and Kent, with the Channel Tunnel just one hour's drive away. There are interesting castles and gardens to visit nearby, including Bodiam, Sissinghurst and Batemans and numerous antique shops to explore in neighbouring picturesque villages. Truly a magical place to while away a few days.

DINING: The Orangery Restaurant has recently been awarded a second AA Rosette for its consistent high quality cuisine and excellent service. Lunch, dinner, afternoon Sussex cream teas and morning coffee are served every day.

Site: ✿ P Payment: 💳 Leisure: ⌇ Property: ⓑ 🍽 🖥 🍴 ⌀ Catering: ⓧ 🍷 Room: 🔌 ♨ 📺 📀

DRAKES HOTEL

43 Marine Parade, Brighton, East Sussex BN2 1PE
T: (01273) 696934 F: (01273) 684805
E: info@drakesofbrighton.com W: www.drakesofbrighton.com

When the stunning double-fronted Regency townhouse was sympathetically renovated to form Drakes, a luxurious, contemporary boutique hotel, they immediately set the standards for style and quality in Brighton and soon established an award winning fine-dining restaurant. All rooms benefit from free Wi-Fi, air conditioning, plasma screen television, iPod docking, free sky (SKY) package and room service. With international experience and exceptional standards, the Restaurant at Drakes has succeeded in achieving several accolades, including the highest score of all Brighton restaurants in the 2015 Good Food Guide, for the sixth consecutive year. Modern European menus are created using only the finest, seasonal ingredients and a comprehensive list offers exceptional old and new world wines to compliment the cuisine. Private dining room/meeting room available.

DINING: 3 course table d'hôte dinner £45pp; 5 course Chef's Taster menu £60pp; lunch & diets available; last orders 2145; breakfast from 0730.

BEDROOMS: 20
Most guest rooms boast impressive sea views and some have fabulous free standing baths. Hand made beds are draped in velvet throws with goose down duvets and pillows to ensure a perfect night's sleep.

ADDITIONAL INFORMATION:
Single, room only, from £125; double from £145. Luxury Gourmet Break: 5 course dinner, b&b from £240 for 2 people sharing.

Site: P Payment: ⊞ Property: ⊛ ♀ 🖥 🅗 ◗ Children: 🏃 🛏 Catering: 🍴 ☂ 🍽
Room: 🔌 🚿 📞 📷 📺 📀

FLACKLEY ASH HOTEL

BEDROOMS: 45
All bedrooms and suites are beautifully furnished and well equipped. Choice of traditional, character rich rooms or more modern, spacious rooms.

B&B PER ROOM PER NIGHT:
S: £95.00 - £169.00
D: £105.00 - £180.00

ADDITIONAL INFORMATION:
Open all year.

Main Street, Peasmarsh, Near Rye, East Sussex TN31 6YH
T: (01797) 230651 **F:** (01797) 230510
E: enquiries@flackleyashhotel.co.uk **W:** www.flackleyashhotel.co.uk

This is one of Sussex' most charming country house hotels. It has an indoor swimming pool and leisure complex, with hydro pool, gym, steam room, saunas, aromatherapy, beauticians and games lawn. The Georgian house radiates a warm and friendly atmosphere, with individually decorated bedrooms. Owners, the Betteridge family, ensure a quality stay for business and leisure guests alike. Rye is only a few miles away with its many historical buildings including the 15th century church, the Ypres Tower, the famous Landgate and Henry James' Georgian residence, Lamb House. There is plenty to do in the area, with antique shops, potteries, local crafts and boutiques and a Thursday market. The fellow Cinque Port, Winchelsea, is nearby, as is Camber Sands, with its beautiful beach and safe bathing. In addition there are famous castles, abbeys and gardens to visit.

DINING: À la carte menu. Dining by candlelight in the conservatory or overlooking the hotel's gardens, the restaurant boasts menus using the finest local produce.

Site: ✿ P **Payment:** 💷 **Leisure:** ▶ ⚘ ⚔ ♨ ⚓ **Property:** ⚐ 🐾 🖼 **Children:** 🐕 **Catering:** (✕ 🍷 **Room:** 🔌 ♨ 📺 📀

MILLSTREAM HOTEL

Bosham Lane, Bosham, Bosham Nr Chichester, West Sussex PO18 8HL
T: (01243) 573234 **F:** (01243) 573459
E: info@millstreamhotel.com **W:** www.millstreamhotel.com

The Millstream is situated in the heart of old Bosham, an historic village with a fine Saxon church on the shores of Chichester Harbour. It combines the elegance of a small English country house with the character and charm of an 18th century malthouse cottage. The restaurant, overlooking the gardens, has two AA Rosettes and is renowned for its excellent cuisine, it offers a selection of English and European dishes. A more casual Brasserie was opened in Summer 2012. The charming sitting room, with its deep-cushioned armchairs, grand piano, bowls of freshly cut flowers and tranquil atmosphere, is the ideal place to meet up with friends over afternoon tea or an aperitif, play cards or just relax with a good novel or magazine. At one point the garden is bisected by an eponymous Millstream which flows past the gazebo. Bosham is a perfect centre from which to explore this area of outstanding natural beauty and historical interest.

DINING: 3 course table d'hôte dinner £35.50; special diets available; last orders 2100; breakfast from 0730.

BEDROOMS: 35
Each bedroom is different and there are two suites across the bridge in the thatched "Waterside Cottage".

B&B PER ROOM PER NIGHT:
S: £99.00 - £109.00
D: £159.00 - £229.00

ADDITIONAL INFORMATION:
Open all year.

Site: ❀ Payment: 💳 Leisure: 🚲 Property: 🍴 📺 ◐ Children: 🐴 Catering: 🍽 🍷 🍲 Room: 📶 ♿ 📞

London

LONDON

Grand landmarks, gorgeous gardens, spectacular shopping, exciting attractions, museums, galleries, theatres, sporting venues and all the buzz and history of the capital - London's treasures are beyond measure. A single trip is never enough and you'll find yourself returning time and again to take in the many unforgettable sights and experiences on offer.

LONDON

In the Central/West End area the most visited sights are the now public rooms of Buckingham Palace, the National Gallery in Trafalgar Square, Tate Britain on Millbank, Westminster Abbey, Houses of Parliament and Cabinet War Rooms.

Westminster Abbey, nearly a thousand years old, has tombs of many English kings, queens, statesmen and writers. The British Museum in Bloomsbury houses one of the world's largest selections of antiquities, including the Magna Carta, the Elgin Marbles and the first edition of Alice in Wonderland. This entire area can be well viewed from The London Eye on the South Bank.

No visit to London is complete without a spot of shopping. Head for bustling Oxford Street and the stylish shops on Regent Street and Bond Street, or check out the trendy boutiques around Carnaby Street.

National Gallery
Westminster WC2N 5DN
(020) 7747 2888
www.nationalgallery.org.uk
The National Gallery houses one of the greatest collections of Western European painting in the world. Discover inspiring art by Botticelli, Caravaggio, Leonardo da Vinci, Monet, Raphael, Rembrandt, Titian, Vermeer and Van Gogh.

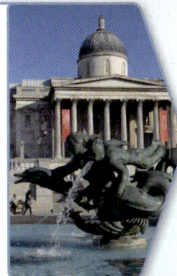

Heading east, St Pauls Cathedral in the city of London was redesigned by Sir Christopher Wren and the nearby the Tower of London, a medieval fortress dominated by the White Tower and dating from 1097, houses The Crown Jewels, guarded by the famous Beefeaters. Even further east, the Queen Elizabeth Olympic Park is the exciting legacy of the 2012 Olympic Games and is situated at the heart of a new, vibrant East London. The main stadium re-opens in October 2015 for the Rugby World Cup, before being permanently transformed into the national centre for athletics in the UK and the new home of West Ham United Football Club.

For entertainment, enjoy a wide range of theatre, bars, restaurants and culture in Covent Garden and don't forget to take in a musical or an off-beat play and the amazing nightime atmosphere around Leicester Square. Madame Tussauds features all your favourite celebrities and super heroes, or if you fancy an historical fright, visit the London Dungeon near Tower Bridge or explore the streets of old London on a Jack the Ripper tour.

London's parks are its lungs. St James, the oldest, was founded by Henry VIII in 1532. Hyde Park, bordering Kensington, Mayfair and Marylebone, is the largest at 630 acres and one of the greatest city parks in the world. You can enjoy any number of outdoor activities, visit the Serpentine Galleries for contemporary art or Speakers' Corner, the most famous location for free speech in the world. Regents Park, with its zoo, lies north of Oxford Circus and was given to the nation by the Prince Regent.

Natural History Museum
Kensington and Chelsea SW7 5BD
(020) 7942 5000 • www.nhm.ac.uk
The Natural History Museum reveals how the jigsaw of life fits together. Animal, vegetable or mineral, the best of our planet's most amazing treasures are here for you to see - for free.

To the South East of the capital, Canary Wharf is one of London's main financial centres and on the south bank, opposite Docklands, attractions include the National Maritime Museum incorporating the Royal Greenwich Observatory, the Cutty Sark and The O2, one of London's premier entertainment venues.

On Saturday 14th November 2015, the 800th Lord Mayors Show will feature a parade of over 6,000 people, military marching bands, acrobats, a procession of decorated floats, a gilded State Coach in which the Lord Mayor travels and starts with an RAF flypast. After the procession London's City Guides will be on hand to lead free guided tours of the City's more strange and wonderful corners, and in the evening fireworks will light up the sky over the river. Visit their website for more information.www.lordmayorsshow.org.

London Transport Museum
Westminster WC2E 7BB
(020) 7379 6344
www.ltmuseum.co.uk
The history of transport for everyone, from spectacular vehicles, special exhibitions, actors and guided tours to film shows, gallery talks and children's craft workshops.

HUDSON'S HISTORIC HOUSES & GARDENS HIGHLIGHTS

575 Wandsworth Road
(020) 7720 9459
www.nationaltrust.org.uk
The hand carved fretwork of this modest early 19th Century house terraced house is enthralling and inspiring.

Chiswick House
(020) 8742 3905
www.chgt.org.uk
Chiswick House is a magnificent neo-Palladian villa set in 65 acres of beautiful historic gardens.

Houses of Parliament
(020) 7219 4114
www.parliament.uk/visiting
Inside one of London's most iconic buildings, tours of the Houses of Parliament offer visitors a unique combination of one thousand years of history, modern day politics, and stunning art and architecture.

Kensington Palace
(0844) 482 7777
www.hrp.org.uk/kensingtonpalace
Discover stories from Queen Victoria's life in her own words. Follow the footsteps of courtiers from the past. Explore the new landscaped gardens, inspired by the famous lawns that existed in the 18th century.

Osterley Park and House
(020) 8232 5050
www.nationaltrust.org.uk/osterley
Created in the late 18th century by architect Robert Adam, Osterley is one of the last surviving country estates in London.

Spencer House
(020) 7514 1958
www.spencerhouse.co.uk
London's most magnificent 18th century private palace.

Strawberry Hill House
(020) 8744 1241
www.strawberryhillhouse.org.uk
Strawberry Hill House is Britain's finest example of Gothic Revival architecture and interior decoration.

Sutton House
(020) 8986 2264
www.nationaltrust.org.uk/suttonhouse
Built in 1535 for Henry VIII, with 18th Century additions. Peel back the layers of time and discover some unexpected occupants.

Tower of London
(0844) 482 7777
www.hrp.org.uk/toweroflondon
The ancient stones reverberate with dark secrets, priceless jewels glint in fortified vaults and pampered ravens strut the grounds.

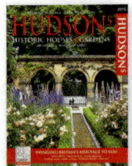

For more suggestions of great historic days out across Britain visit
www.hudsonsheritage.com

LONDON
WHERE TO STAY

Entries appear alphabetically by town name in each county.

A key to symbols appears on page 4.

SEARCYS ROOF GARDEN ROOMS

30 Pavilion Road, London, Greater London SW1X 0HJ
T: (020) 7584 4921 **F:** (020) 7823 8694
E: rgr@searcys.co.uk **W:** www.searcys.co.uk

Searcys Roof Garden Rooms at 30 Pavilion Road provides a peaceful haven in the heart of Knightsbridge. It offers a relaxed atmosphere and friendly staff with a high level of personal and attentive service. The beautiful boutique bedrooms in this Georgian style townhouse boast an unusual breed of charm and character. All 11 rooms are individually designed to have a country house feel, however now with super kingsize beds, plasma TV's with a wide option of channels, plus our usual amenities, such as, Wi-Fi, air conditioning and tea and coffee brought automatically to your room. Bathrooms provide luxury touches with bath robes and Molton Brown products. This hotel is a hidden gem in the bustle of London, yet conveniently located for Knightsbridge, Hyde Park, museums and the theatre district. It is perfect for people seeking an alternative to large hotel chains.

DINING: The Roof Terrace is the ideal area to take breakfast on a sunny morning or to finish your day off with a glass of chilled wine. 24 hour room service.

BEDROOMS: 11
All 11 rooms are individually designed to have a country house feel, however now with super kingsize beds, plasma TV's with a wide option of channels.

B&B PER ROOM PER NIGHT:
S: £155.00 - £169.00
D: £239.00 - £258.00

ADDITIONAL INFORMATION:
Closed during Christmas.

Site: ✿ **Payment:** 💳 **Property:** ⊛ ⍓ 🖥 🖨 🎀 ◐ **Children:** 🐾 🛏 **Room:** 🔌 💧 📞 📺 📀

SAN DOMENICO HOUSE

BEDROOMS: 17

The bedrooms are very differently decorated; each of them individually themed and furnished with lovely antiques. They are all air-conditioned, have an individually stocked minibar, flat screen TVs, DVD players and their own stylish bathroom facilities with Molton Brown toiletries and hand made olive oil beauty products and fluffy bathrobes.

ADDITIONAL INFORMATION:
Open all year.

29-31 Draycott Place, London, Greater London SW3 2SH
T: (020) 7581 5757 **F:** (020) 7584 1348
E: info@sandomenicohouse.com **W:** www.sandomenicohouse.com

San Domenico House is an intimate, luxurious "boutique" townhouse hotel located only a few minutes walk from bustling Sloane Square and the fashionable heart of Chelsea. Behind its Victorian facade, San Domenico House enjoys all the luxuries of a small palace preserving the charm and intimacy of its 17 rooms and suites. With easy access to the city and West End, it is ideally suited to business executives and leisure travellers alike. Free WiFi internet connection is provided in all bedrooms.

An additional feature is a rooftop terrace with far-reaching views across Chelsea. Whether guests want to have an English or Continental breakfast in the charming breakfast room or they wish to enjoy afternoon tea in the antiques-filled lounge, San Domenico House will provide them with the highest standard of service in a comfortable and relaxed atmosphere.

DINING: Breakfast only but room service available.

AA ★★★★★ Guest House

Site: ✿ Payment: 💷 Property: 🖥 🏠 Catering: ⚔ 🍷 Room: 📞 🌐 📺 📀

THE MAYFLOWER

26-28 Trebovir Road, London, Greater London SW5 9NJ
T: (020) 7370 0991 **F:** (020) 7370 0994
E: info@mayflower-group.co.uk **W:** www.themayflowerhotel.co.uk

This well established independently run hotel is close to Earls Court Exhibition Centre, Olympia and the Underground providing a fast link to the West End. The Mayflower is a sister hotel to Twenty Nevern Square and has just completed an extensive refurbishment to bring it up to 4 star standard. With the introduction of a lounge/coffee bar, a smart new reception area and an enhanced breakfast room, guests will feel immediately at home. Secure parking can be arranged. The studios and apartments are for longer term occupation and come with daily maid service, fully equipped kitchens, bathrooms and entry phone system. We recommend The Mayflower as a homely place with friendly and attentive multi-lingual staff.

DINING: Continental breakfast is included in the room rate. No food is served beyond this but the coffee bar is open until 6pm.

BEDROOMS: 48
Individually themed bedrooms and suites.

B&B PER ROOM PER NIGHT:
S: £69.00 - £109.00
D: £79.00 - £199.00

ADDITIONAL INFORMATION:
Double room types: Executive, Four poster and Luxury. Triple, family and suites are available. Sunday to Wednesday discounts are available, subject to availability. Season and event specials too.

AA
★★★★
Hotel

Site: P Payment: 💳 € **Property:** 🚭 🍴 ◐ **Children:** 🐴 **Room:** 🛜 💧 📞 📺 🔌 🧺

TWENTY NEVERN SQUARE

BEDROOMS: 20
Individually appointed bedrooms
and suites.

B&B PER ROOM PER NIGHT:
D: £120.00 - £260.00

ADDITIONAL INFORMATION:
Minimum prices: Luxury doubles from
£120; Luxury 4 posters from £149;
Suites from £180. Weekly and event
specials run, subject to availability.

20 Nevern Square, London SW5 9PD
T: (020) 7565 9555 **F:** (020) 7370 0994
E: hotel@twentynevernsquare.co.uk **W:** www.twentynevernsquare.co.uk

Overlooking a quiet, tree-lined garden square, this is one of London's newest and, at the same time, most original and discreet boutique hotels. The mosaic patterned steps of the late 19th century mansion give a hint of the Eastern influences within, which are also apparent in the decor of the cosy ground floor lounge. The interior has been refurbished in exotic style. Most impressive are the carved oriental headboards and wardrobes and the silk curtains, found in, for example, The Grand Pasha Suite or the Chinese Room. The sleek marble bathrooms, too, imitate those found in designer hotels. The eastern feel extends to the lounge and light, airy conservatory / breakfast room, which is filled with wicker furniture and greenery. The hotel is close to Earls Court and Olympia Exhibition Centres and has easy access to the West End, Kensington, Chelsea and Knightsbridge. To stay in this distinctive townhouse hotel is an experience not to be missed.

DINING: Continental breakfast is included in the room rate. In room dining menu available from 5pm to midnight.

Site: ⚑ P **Payment:** 🖃 € **Property:** 🍴 🖥 🗄 🛏 ◑ **Children:** ➣ **Catering:** ⦂X 🍴 🍽
Room: ☎ 📺 🛁 🖨

THE NEW LINDEN

59 Leinster Square, London, Greater London W2 4PS
T: (020) 7221 4321 **F:** (020) 7727 3156
E: newlindenhotel@mayflower-group.co.uk **W:** www.newlindenhotel.co.uk

New Linden has recently undergone a major refurbishment to bring it up to the level of a top standard townhouse hotel. The displays of seasonal flowers outside welcome the visitor to the hotel, a recent winner of a London in Bloom award. There is the usual range of rooms of varying shapes and sizes, all attractively furnished and comfortable with gleaming bathroom or shower areas. Broad darkwood headboards add an original touch. Two strikingly unusual family rooms in terms of size and layout sleep up to five, one of these being on split levels with Doric columns dividing the upper and lower sections. A spacious breakfast room in the basement serves an extensive continental buffet to guests. The New Linden enjoys a quiet location in Leinster Square with Queensway and Bayswater underground stations both within five minutes walk, and Paddington station & the Heathrow Express 15 minutes walk away. The area is cosmopolitan with a varied choice of restaurants and Whiteleys, the indoor shopping mall, close by.

DINING: Continental breakfast is included in the room rate. In-room dining menu is available from 1700 - 0100.

BEDROOMS: 50
Individually appointed bedrooms and suites.

B&B PER ROOM PER NIGHT:
S: £85.00 - £125.00
D: £125.00 - £150.00

ADDITIONAL INFORMATION:
Additional room types: Suites from £169; Family rooms from £249. Discounted rates available Sunday to Thursday (subject to availability). Valentines, Christmas, New Year and Honeymoon specials (STA).

AA ★★★★ Hotel

Site: ✱ Payment: 💳 Property: 🖥 📠 🌙 Children: 🧸 Room: ✋ 📞 📺 📺 🔌 🛏

Norfolk

Huntingdonshire

Cambridgeshire   Suffolk

Bedfordshire

Essex

Hertfordshire

EAST OF ENGLAND
Bedfordshire, Cambridgeshire, Essex, Hertfordshire, Norfolk, Suffolk

Loved for its unspoiled character, rural landscape, architecture and traditions, the East of England is full of beautiful countryside, idyllic seaside, historic cities and vibrant towns. The Norfolk Broads and Suffolk Coast have always been popular with yachtsmen and the North Norfolk Coast has become a fashionable getaway in recent years. Cambridge is steeped in history and oozes sophistication, while Bedfordshire, Hertfordshire and Essex each have their own charms, with pockets of beauty and fascinating heritage. This is a diverse region where you'll find plenty to keep you busy.

EAST OF ENGLAND

BEDFORDSHIRE & HERTFORDSHIRE

History, the arts, family entertainment and relaxing, unspoilt countryside - this area has it all. Bedfordshire has plenty of attractions, from exotic animals at Whipsnade Zoo to vintage aeroplanes at The Shuttleworth Collection and notable historic houses. Woburn Abbey, the still inhabited home of the Dukes of Bedford, stands in a 3000-acre park and is part of one of Europe's largest drive-through game reserves. The 18th century mansion's 14 state apartments are open to the public and contain an impressive art collection. Luton Hoo is a fine Robert Adam designed house in a 1200-acre Capability Brown designed park.

Hertfordshire also has its fair share of stately homes, with Hatfield House, built from 1707 by Robert Cecil, first Earl of Salisbury, leading the way. Nearby Knebworth House is the venue for popular summer concerts and events.

Roman walls, mosaic floors and part of an amphitheatre are still visible at Verulanium, St Albans and Much Hadham, where the Bishops of London used to have their country seat, is a showpiece village. Welwyn Garden City, one of Britain's first 20th century new towns retains a certain art deco charm.

Western Essex is dotted with pretty historic market towns and villages like Thaxted and Saffron Walden and plenty of historic sites. County town Colchester was founded by the Romans and its massive castle keep, built in 1067 on the site of the Roman Temple of Claudius, houses a collection of Roman antiquities. Explore the beautiful gardens and 110ft Norman Keep at Hedingham Castle, which also holds jousting and theatre performances.

Audley End House & Gardens
Saffron Walden, Essex CB11 4JF
www.english-heritage.org.uk
Discover one of England's grandest stately homes. Explore the impressive mansion house, uncover the story behind the Braybrooke's unique natural history collection, visit an exhibition about the workers who lived on the estate in the 1800s and even try dressing the part with dressing up clothes provided.

CAMBRIDGESHIRE & ESSEX

Cambridge is a city of winding streets lined with old houses, world-famous colleges and churches, while the gently flowing Cam provides a serene backdrop to the architectural wonders. Kings College Chapel, started by Henry VI in 1446 should not be missed and the Fitzwilliam Museum is one of Europe's treasure houses, with antiquities from Greece and Rome. First-class shopping can be found in the quirky stores and exquisite boutiques tucked away along cobbled streets, and there's a vast choice of places to eat and drink.

Further afield, Cambridgeshire is a land of lazy waterways, rolling countryside, bustling market towns and quaint villages. Climb grand sweeping staircases in the stately homes of the aristocracy or relax as you chug along in a leisure boat, watching the wildlife in one of the wonderful nature reserves. Peterborough has a fine Norman cathedral with three soaring arches, whilst Ely has had an abbey on its cathedral site since AD 670.

Some of the region's loveliest countryside lies to the north, on the Suffolk Border around Dedham Vale where Constable and Turner painted, while further east you can find family seaside resorts such as Walton on the Naze and Clacton-on-Sea. Following the coast south, the Blackwater and Crouch estuaries provide havens for yachts and pleasure craft. Inland, Layer Marney Tower is a Tudor palace with buildings, gardens and parkland dating from 1520 in a beautiful, rural Essex setting. The county city of Chelmsford has a historic 15th century cathedral and Hylands House is a beautiful Grade II* listed neo-classical villa, set in over 500 acres of Hylands Park.

NORFOLK

Norfolk is not as flat as you might think, but cycling or walking is still a great way to see the county. In the west Thetford Forest is said to be the oldest in England while in the east, the county is crisscrossed by waterways and lakes known as The Broads - apparently the remains of medieval man's peat diggings!

The county town of Norfolk and unofficial capital of East Anglia is Norwich, a fine city whose cathedral walls are decorated with biblical scenes dating from 1046. There are 30 medieval churches in central Norwich and many other interesting historic sites, but modern Norwich is a stylish contemporary city with first rate shopping and cultural

facilities. Sandringham, near Kings Lynn in the north west of the county, is the royal palace bought by Queen Victoria for the then Prince of Wales and where the present Queen spends many a family holiday.

The North Norfolk coast has become known as 'Chelsea-on-Sea' in recent years and many parts of the region have developed a reputation for fine dining. From Hunstanton in the west to Cromer in the east, this stretch of coastline is home to nature reserves, windswept beaches and quaint coastal villages. Wells-next-the-Sea, with its long sweeping beach bordered by pine woodland has a pretty harbour with small fishing boats where children fish for crabs.

Holkham Hall
Wells-next- the-Sea, Norfolk, NR23 1AB
(01328) 710227
www.holkham.co.uk
Steeped in history, magnificent Holkham Hall on the North Norfolk Coast, is a stunning Palladian mansion with its own nature reserve. It is home to many rare species of flora and fauna, a deer park and one of the most beautiful, unspoilt beaches in the country.

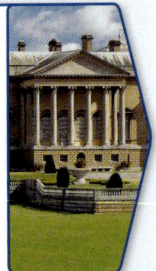

SUFFOLK

Suffolk is famous for its winding lanes and pastel painted, thatched cottages. The county town of Ipswich has undergone considerable regeneration in recent years, and now boasts a vibrant waterfront and growing arts scene. For history lovers, Framlingham Castle has stood intact since the 13th century and magnificent churches at Lavenham, Sudbury and Long Melford are well worth a visit.

The Suffolk Coast & Heaths Area of Outstanding Natural Beauty has 155 square miles of unspoilt wildlife-rich wetlands, ancient heaths, windswept shingle beaches and historic towns and villages for you to explore. Its inlets and estuaries are extremely popular with yachtsmen. Gems such as Southwold, with its brightly coloured beach huts, and Aldeburgh are home to some excellent restaurants. Snape Maltings near Aldeburgh offers an eclectic programme of events including the world famous Aldeburgh Festival of music. The historic market town of Woodbridge on the River Deben, has a working tide mill, a fabulous riverside walk with an impressive view across the river to Sutton Hoo and an abundance of delightful pubs and restaurants.

In the south of the county, the hills and valleys on the Suffolk-Essex border open up to stunning skies, captured in paintings by Constable, Turner and Gainsborough. At the heart of beautiful Constable Country, Nayland and Dedham Vale Area of Outstanding Natural Beauty are idyllic places for a stroll or leisurely picnic.

Somerleyton Hall and Gardens
Lowestoft, Suffolk NR32 5QQ
(01502) 734901
www.somerleyton.co.uk
12 acres of landscaped gardens to explore including our famous 1864 Yew hedge maze. Guided tours of the Hall.

HUDSON'S HISTORIC HOUSES & GARDENS HIGHLIGHTS

Benington Lordship Gardens
(01438) 869668
www.beningtonlordship.co.uk
7 acre garden overlooking lakes.
Features include Norman Keep, moat,
Queen Anne manor house, formal
rose garden and verandah.

Brentwood Cathedral
(01277) 232266
www.cathedral-brentwood.org
The new Roman Catholic classical
Cathedral Church of St Mary and St
Helen incorporates part of the original
Victorian Church.

Copped Hall
(020) 7267 1679
www.coppedhalltrust.org.uk
Mid 18th Century Palladian Mansion
currently undergoing restoration. Former
elaborate gardens also being rescued.

Elton Hall
(01832) 280468
www.eltonhall.com
A fascinating mixture of styles and
every room contains treasures -
magnificent furniture and fine paintings
from early 15th Century Old Masters.

Hatfield House
(01707) 287010
www.hatfield-house.co.uk
Over 400 years of culture, history
and entertainment.

Hindringham Hall and Gardens
(01328) 878226
www.hindringhamhall.org
Beautiful Tudor Manor house
surrounded by 12th Century moat.
A scheduled ancient monument with
3 acres of fishponds.

Houghton Hall & Gardens
(01485) 528569
www.houghtonhall.com
Houghton Hall is one of the finest
examples of Palladian architecture
in England. Built in 18th century
by Sir Robert Walpole, Britain's first
Prime Minister.

Oxburgh Hall
(01366) 328258
www.nationaltrust.org.uk
A romantic, moated manor house
built by the Bedingfeld family in the
15th century, they have lived here
ever since.

Peckover House & Gardens NT
(01945) 583463
www.nationaltrust.org.uk/peckover
Peckover House is an oasis hidden
away in an urban environment.
A classic Georgian merchant's
townhouse, it was lived in by the
Peckover family for 150 years and
reflects the Quaker lifestyle.

Woburn Abbey
(01525) 290333
www.woburnabbey.co.uk
Visit the home of Afternoon Tea to
enjoy priceless treasures, uncover
fascinating stories, and explore the
beautiful gardens.

HUDSON'S
HISTORIC HOUSES & GARDENS
MUSEUMS & HERITAGE SITES

For more suggestions
of great historic days
out across Britain visit
www.hudsonsheritage.com

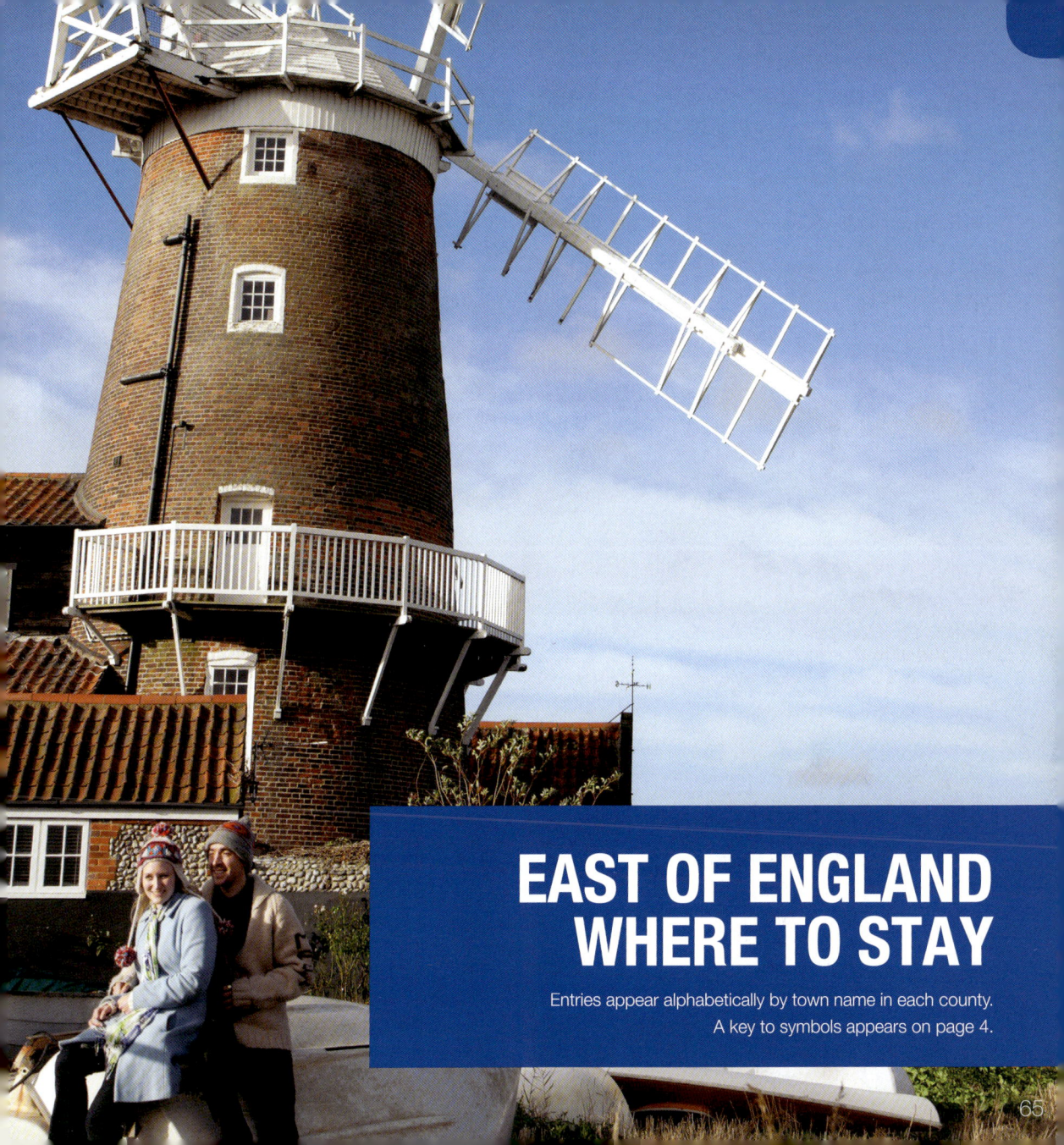

EAST OF ENGLAND
WHERE TO STAY

Entries appear alphabetically by town name in each county.
A key to symbols appears on page 4.

MAISON TALBOOTH

Stratford Road, Dedham, Colchester, Essex CO7 6HN
T: (01206) 322367 **F:** (01206) 322752
E: maison@milsomhotels.com **W:** www.milsomhotels.com/maisontalbooth

Maison Talbooth is a Victorian house which has been owned by the Milsom family for over 40 years and is now one of the leading hotels of East Anglia. It is situated on the Essex/Suffolk border, ½ mile from the picturesque village of Dedham and overlooking the beautiful Dedham Vale, famous Constable country. The top floor has a Spa with two double treatment rooms. As well as a tennis court, there is a swimming pool in the grounds, with changing rooms and showers, decked area and a hot tub. Guests can enjoy a cocktail or snack lunch by the pool, relax by a log fire or enjoy an evening barbecue. There is also a beautifully appointed Garden Room and an all weather tennis court is nearby. Serious eating happens at Le Talbooth, the two AA Rosette restaurant nearby. This 16th century timber framed building was formerly a toll booth. It overlooks the river Stour and private rooms can be hired. Outside one can sit under an architectural Sail or wander in the large garden.

DINING: Average three course à la carte £50 pp. Open every day for lunch and dinner excluding Sunday evenings.

BEDROOMS: 12
12 double.

B&B PER ROOM PER NIGHT:
D: £230.00 - £425.00

ADDITIONAL INFORMATION:
Spa breaks and family breaks available. See website. An idyllic setting for weddings and functions.

Site: ❀ P **Payment:** 💳 **Leisure:** ♪ ▸ ✕ ⋈ ⤫ ⚲ **Property:** ⚶ 🐕 🚬 🗄 ⨝ ⌀ **Children:** 🐕 🛏 🚶
Catering: (✕ ⚱ 🍽 **Room:** ✶ 🔟 📺 🆅 🗲

THE PIER AT HARWICH

BEDROOMS: 14
Seven of the en suite bedrooms are in the main building, seven in the adjacent Angel, all very attractive with a nautical flavour and panoramic sea views.

B&B PER ROOM PER NIGHT:
D: £125.00 - £200.00

ADDITIONAL INFORMATION:
Fishing and sailing trips can be arranged, as can trips to see the seals on the Walton backwaters. Harwich is also the home of the Mayflower.

The Quay, Harwich, Essex CO12 3HH
T: (01255) 241212 **F:** (01225) 551922
E: pier@milsomhotels.com **W:** www.milsomhotels.com/thepier

The Pier was built in 1862 in the style of a Venetian palazzo to provide overnight accommodation for passengers travelling by train and ship to the Continent. The Great Eastern Railway's terminal was the Ha'Penny Pier (the cost of entry in those days). Gerald Milsom bought the Pier in 1978 and opened a seafood restaurant. It is wonderfully situated on the seafront overlooking the harbour at the confluence of the Stour and Orwell rivers. Across the water is Shotley Yacht Marina with Felixstowe in the distance. Yachts and boats can be chartered from the hotel by arrangement. The visitors dine in a most attractive brasserie. The ambience is rustic but comfortable with scrubbed floors, Farrow & Ball paintwork, framed posters and wooden mirrors. Diners jot down their orders on a notepad and hand them to one of the helpful staff. An elegant wooden staircase leads to the two AA Rosette Harbourside restaurant on the first floor. The restaurant with its fine views over the twin estuaries of the Stour and Orwell takes its influence from the sea.

DINING: 2 restaurants - Harbourside 2 AA Rosettes closed on a Monday & Tuesday. Ha'penny Bistro open all day, every day.
Site: P Payment: ⊞ **Leisure:** ⊁ **Property:** ⚓ ⛵ ☰ ♨ ◑ **Catering:** ⟨✕ ⟐ ⟐
Room: 🔌 ✦ 📞 📻 📺 ☕ ♨

THE NORFOLK MEAD HOTEL

Church Loke, Coltishall, Norwich, Norfolk NR12 7DN
T: (01603) 737531
E: info@norfolkmead.co.uk **W:** www.norfolkmead.co.uk

Anna & James Holliday took over The Norfolk Mead in early 2013 and have transformed the hotel, winning several awards for cuisine and hospitality. There are 13 contemporarily refurbished bedrooms in the main building, there is also the Crab Apple Suite, a converted Summer House and Sweet Chestnut Cottage in the grounds, which sleeps up to four. James and Anna both come from catering backgrounds and Anna, who is the hard working chef, also runs Anna Duttson Events, catering for outside events and receptions. The 'Garden Room' opened in the grounds in 2014 and can cater for up to 150 wedding or meeting guests. The AA Rosette menu, which changes monthly, uses local produce wherever possible. We had pan seared scallops with puy lentils, followed by a duo of spring lamb, slow cooked shoulder and lamb cutlets, with a delicious baked lemon cheesecake and fruit compote to finish. Breakfast was equally delicious with home baked bread, jams and cereals and the Mead is also developing a reputation for afternoon teas.

DINING: À la carte & special diets available; last orders 2100; breakfast from 0730.

Site: ❀ **P** **Payment:** 🖃 **Leisure:** ♪ ⚲ ⚴ **Property:** 🐾 🐕 ⊟ ⛱ ⌀ **Children:** ⛷ 🛏 🛝
Catering: (✗ ⚱ 🍽 **Room:** 🍷 ✿ ☎ 📺

BEDROOMS: 13
The 13 contemporarily refurbished bedrooms are named after hedgerow plants and herbs which can be foraged for in Norfolk; Samphire, Mulberry, Hawthorn, Sorrel and so on. Three suites have free standing baths in the rooms and the other nine have large 'rain' showers.

B&B PER ROOM PER NIGHT:
S: £130.00 - £190.00
D: £130.00 - £190.00

ADDITIONAL INFORMATION:
Dinner, b&b £180 – £240.00 per double room; Sweet Chestnut Cottage from £245.00.

AA
★★★★
Country House
Hotel

BROOM HALL COUNTRY HOTEL

BEDROOMS: 15
Bedrooms are spacious and airy with pretty bedspreads and most have views over the grounds.

B&B PER ROOM PER NIGHT:
S: £75.00 - £95.00
D: £85.00 - £165.00

ADDITIONAL INFORMATION:
Two of the five cheerful ground floor rooms in the converted stable block are suitable for disabled access. The air-conditioned conference room can double as a ballroom.

Richmond Road, Saham Toney, Watton, Norfolk IP25 7EX
T: (01953) 882125 **F:** (01953) 885325
E: enquiries@broomhallhotel.co.uk **W:** www.broomhallhotel.co.uk

Broom Hall is a family-run Victorian country house set in 15 acres of garden and parkland in the peaceful West Norfolk countryside. The traditional English gardens are laid out with mixed and herbaceous borders and mature trees to provide a welcome oasis of colour and fragrance in which guests can relax. New refurbished reception rooms retain ornate moulded ceilings. There is an indoor heated swimming pool. The whole house can be hired for a special occasion. Within easy driving distance are Sandringham and Blickling Hall. Thetford Forest Park and the trans-Norfolk Peddars Way. Dining is either in the Swallowtails fine dining restaurant or alternaively the Ivy Room, Conservatory or Terrace, all use fresh local produce where possible and pride themsleves on mouth-watering homemade desserts. Homemade cream teas are another treat.

DINING: 3 course à la carte dinner £21 – £32; lunch & bar snacks available; last orders 2030 hrs.

Site: ✿ P **Payment:** 💷 **Leisure:** ♒ ☂ **Property:** ® ♈ 🐾 ⊟ ◑ ⌕ **Children:** 🧸 ♨ ⚲
Catering: (✗ ♟ 🍴 **Room:** ♨ ⚓ ☏ 📺 ⚙

HINTLESHAM HALL HOTEL

Hintlesham, Ipswich, Suffolk IP8 3NS
T: (01473) 652334 **F:** (01473) 652463
E: reservations@hintleshamhall.com **W:** www.hintleshamhall.com

Hintlesham Hall is one of the loveliest hotels in England. The estate is entered along an impressive tree-lined drive, at the end of which the pale apricot coloured Grade I country house hotel reveals itself. It is set in beautifully maintained, peaceful and mature gardens. Parts of the house date back to the middle of the 15th Century. Décor combines the palatial and the cosy with fine fabrics, works of art and antique furnishings. Guests can relax in the friendly ambience of this superb country house hotel with attentive, friendly staff, award winning fine dining, meeting and conference rooms and an extensive range of beauty treatments. Well placed for exploring Suffolk's delightfully unspoilt 16th century wool merchants' villages, its pretty river estuaries and 'Constable Country'. Newmarket Aldeburgh, Lavenham, Long Melford and Woodbridge are all nearby, with Ipswich's vibrant new waterfront area just four miles away. Hintlesham Hall also offers a variety of local walks or is the perfect retreat for those who just want to relax in gracious surroundings.

DINING: 2 AA Rosette Dining Award. À La Carte & table d'hôte menus available. £33.00 for table d'hôte, last orders at 2100 and breakfast from 0700.
Site: ✿ P **Payment:** 🖃 **Leisure:** ▶ ⋈ ⚲ **Property:** ⊤ ⋔ ▤ 🖾 🖁 ◑ ⌀ **Children:** ⥾ ▦ ⚲
Catering: (✗ ⅄ ⊠ **Room:** ⛾ ⬙ ☏ ⑬ ⑬ ⚱ ⊞

BEDROOMS: 32
Individually designed and luxuriously appointed bedrooms including some with four-poster beds and many with original timber beams.

B&B PER ROOM PER NIGHT:
S: £99.00 - £419.00
D: £99.00 - £419.00

ADDITIONAL INFORMATION:
Sharing the estate is the championship PGA golf course - 18 hole, par 72 layout with preferred green fees for residents and specially tailored breaks. Complimentary Wi-Fi, helipad.

AA
★★★★
Hotel

See front of guide for key to symbols

MILSOMS KESGRAVE HALL

BEDROOMS: 23
Standard, superior, deluxe, principal and 'best' rooms. All are excellent - quiet and luxurious with crisp linen and fluffy towels.

B&B PER ROOM PER NIGHT:
D: £135.00 - £305.00

ADDITIONAL INFORMATION:
There are three private meeting rooms and this year The Hanger has opened in the grounds, with capacity for up to 300 wedding or conference guests. Golf can be arranged at the nearby Felixstowe ferry or Woodbridge courses.

Hall Road, Ipswich, Suffolk IP5 2PU
T: (01473) 333741 **F:** (01473) 617614
E: reception@kesgravehall.com **W:** www.milsomhotels.com/kesgravehall

Kesgrave Hall is a former Grade II Georgian mansion sitting in 38 acres of its own parkland and woodland. It has 23 stylish bedrooms, divided into five categories: standard, superior, deluxe, principal and 'best' rooms. They are opened by a key fob attached to a huge medieval key - not something you are going to walk off with! They are competitively priced and beautifully designed with the latest TVs and MP3 players. The open plan kitchen allows diners to see exactly what is going on. The brasserie style restaurant spills out onto the terrace, which is covered by a vast architectural sail, allowing guests to dine outside in any weather. The menu is imaginative and eclectic, ranging from a tasty sandwich to fresh fish from Harwich and beef from neighbouring Suffolk farms served by cheerful waiting staff. Kesgrave Hall is the perfect base for exploring the Suffolk Heritage Coast and the surrounding towns and villages as well as being a good business base - easily accessible from the A12.

DINING: £25 for 3 courses. Open all day with full menu available from 12 noon.

Site: ⚓ P **Payment:** 💳 **Leisure:** ⚑ **Property:** 🛋 🐕 ♨ 🅱 ♨ ◑ **Children:** 🍼 🛏 ♣ **Catering:** 🍴 🍷 🍽
Room: 🔌 ☕ ☎ 📷 📺 📀 💇

For more fantastic
hotels, special offers,
reviews and news visit
www.signpost.co.uk

Sign up to our monthly
Newsletter for exclusive
hotel offers.

Recommending the UK's Finest Hotels since 1935

www.signpost.co.uk

Lincolnshire

Derbyshire

Nottinghamshire

Rutland
Leicestershire

Northamptonshire

EAST MIDLANDS

Derbyshire, Leicestershire, Lincolnshire, Northamptonshire, Nottinghamshire, Rutland

The East Midlands is a region of historic castles and cathedrals, lavish houses, underground caves, a rich industrial heritage and spectacular countryside including the Peak District and the Lincolnshire Wolds. Climb to enchanting hilltop castles for breathtaking views. Explore medieval ruins and battlefields. Discover hidden walks in ancient forests, cycle across hills and wolds, or visit one of the region's many events and attractions.

EAST MIDLANDS

DERBYSHIRE

'There is no finer county in England than Derbyshire. To sit in the shade on a fine day and look upon verdure is the most perfect refreshment' according to Jane Austen. Derbyshire is the home of the UK's first National Park, the Peak District, which has been popular with holidaymakers for centuries. It forms the beginning of the Pennine Chain and its reservoirs and hills are second to none in beauty. This is excellent walking, riding and cycling country and contains plenty of visitor attractions and historic sites including the 14th century Haddon Hall, Renishaw Hall and Gardens and ruined Ashby-de-la-Zouch castle.

Chatsworth
Bakewell, Derbyshire DE45 1PP
(01246) 565300
www.chatsworth.org
Chatsworth is a spectacular historic house set in the heart of the Peak District in Derbyshire, on the banks of the river Derwent. There are over 30 rooms to explore, including the magnificent Painted Hall and Sculpture Gallery. In the garden, discover water features, giant sculptures and beautiful flowers set in one of Britain's most well-known historic landscapes.

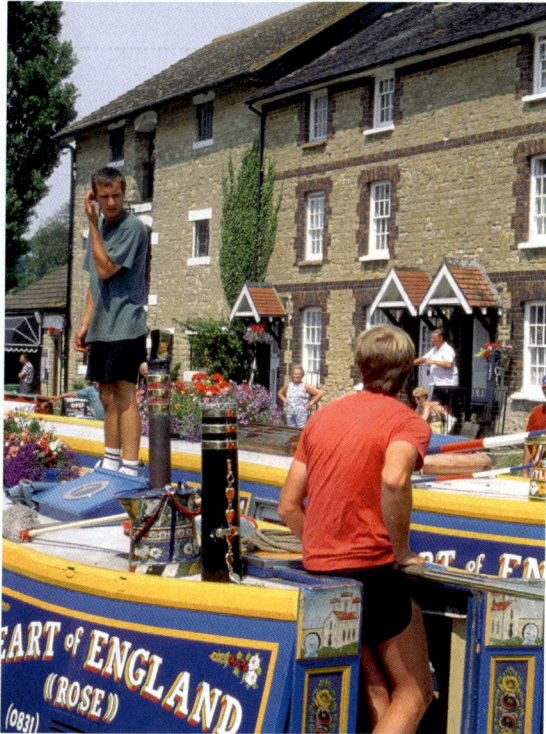

LEICESTERSHIRE & RUTLAND

Leicester is a cathedral city with a 2000-year history, now host to a modern university and the county's pastures fuel one of its main exports: cheese. Foxton Locks is the largest flight of staircase locks on the English canal system with two 'staircases' of five locks bustling with narrowboats. Belvoir Castle in the east dominates its vale. Rockingham Castle at Market Harborough was built by William the Conqueror and stands on the edge of an escarpment giving dramatic views over five counties and the Welland Valley below. Quietly nestling in the English countryside, England's smallest county of Rutland is an idyllic rural destination with an array of unspoilt villages and two charming market towns, packed with rich history and character.

Belvoir Castle
Melton Mowbray,
Leicestershire NG32 1PE
(01476) 871002
www.belvoircastle.com
Home to the Duke and Duchess of Rutland, Belvoir Castle offers stunning views of the Vale of Belvoir.

LINCOLNSHIRE

Lincolnshire is said to produce one eighth of Britain's food and its wide open meadows are testament to this. Gothic triple-towered Lincoln Cathedral is visible from the Fens for miles around, while Burghley House hosts the famous annual Horse Trials and is a top tourist attraction. The Lincolnshire Wolds, a range of hills designated an Area of Outstanding Natural Beauty and the highest area of land in eastern England between Yorkshire and Kent, is idyllic walking and cycling country.

Castle Ashby Gardens
Northamptonshire NN7 1LQ
(01604) 695200
www.castleashbygardens.co.uk
A haven of tranquility and beauty in the heart of Northamptonshire. Take your time to explore these beautiful gardens and enjoy fascinating attractions, from the rare breed farmyard to the historic orangery.

NORTHAMPTONSHIRE

County town Northampton is famous for its shoe making, celebrated in the Central Museum and Art Gallery, and the county also has its share of stately homes and historic battlefields. Silverstone in the south is home to the British Grand Prix. Althorp was the birthplace and is now the resting place of the late Diana Princess of Wales.

Nottingham Castle
Nottingham NG1 6EL
(0115) 915 3700
www.nottinghamcity.gov.uk
Situated on a high rock,
Nottingham Castle commands
spectacular views over the city and
once rivalled the great castles of
Windsor and the Tower of London.

NOTTINGHAMSHIRE

Nottingham's castle dates from 1674 and its Lace Centre
illustrates the source of much of the city's wealth, alongside
other fine examples of Nottinghamshire's architectural
heritage such as Papplewick Hall & Gardens. Legendary
tales of Robin Hood, Sherwood Forest and historic battles
may be what the county is best known for, but it also hosts
world class sporting events, live performances and cutting
edge art, and there's plenty of shopping and fine dining
on offer too. To the north, the remains of Sherwood Forest
provide a welcome breathing space and there are plenty of
country parks and nature reserves, including the beautiful
lakes and landscape of the National Trust's Clumber Park.

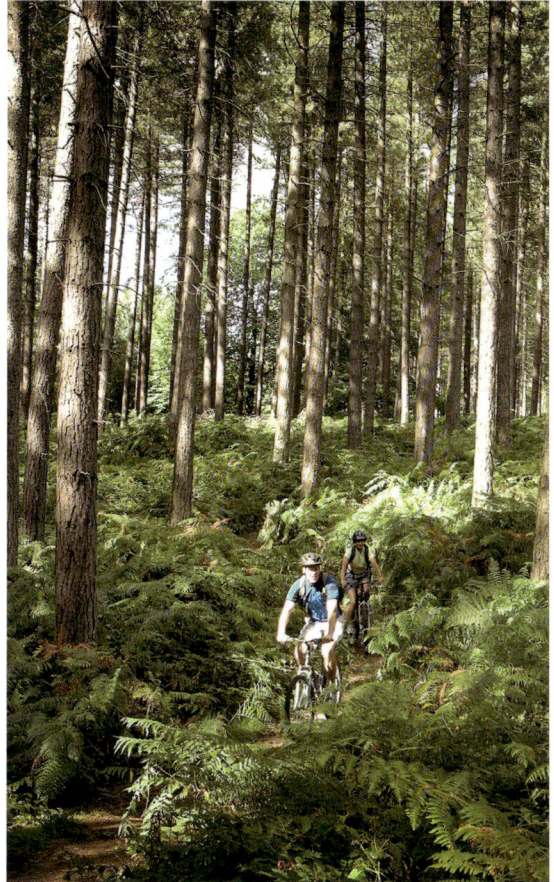

77

HUDSON'S HISTORIC HOUSES & GARDENS HIGHLIGHTS

Burghley House
(01780) 752451
www.burghley.co.uk
Burghley House, home of Cecil family for over 400 years is one of England's greatest Elizabethan houses.

Chatsworth
(01246) 565430
www.chatsworth.org
The home of the Duke and Duchess of Devonshire, Chatsworth is one of the country's greatest Treasure Houses.

Cottesbrooke Hall & Gardens
(01604) 505808
www.cottesbrooke.co.uk
Dating from 1702 the Hall's beauty is matched by the magnificence of the gardens and the excellence of the picture, furniture and porcelain collections.

Deene Park
(01780) 450278
www.deenepark.com
Home of the Brudenell family since 1514, this 16th century house incorporates a medieval manor with important Georgian additions.

Grimsthorpe Castle, Park & Gardens
(01778) 591205
www.grimsthorpe.co.uk
Building styles from 13th century. North front is Vanburgh's last major work. State rooms and picture galleries including tapestries, furniture and paintings.

Haddon Hall
(01629) 812855
www.haddonhall.co.uk
Haddon Hall sits on a rocky outcrop above the river Wye near the market town of Bakewell, looking much as it would have done in Tudor Times.

Holdenby
(01604) 770074
www.holdenby.com
Once the largest private house in England and subsequently the palace of James I and prison of Charles I, Holdenby has recently been seen in the BBC's acclaimed adaptaion of 'Great Expectations'.

Lamport Hall & Gardens
(01604) 686272
www.lamporthall.co.uk
The home of the Isham family for 400 years, Lamport Hall contains an outstanding collection of furniture and paintings.

Rockingham Castle
(01536) 770240
www.rockinghamcastle.com
Rockingham Castle stands on the edge of an escarpment giving dramatic views over five counties and the Welland Valley below. Built by William the Conqueror, the Castle was a royal residence for 450 years.

HUDSON'S
HISTORIC HOUSES & GARDENS
MUSEUMS & HERITAGE SITES

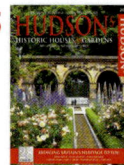

For more suggestions of great historic days out across Britain visit
www.hudsonsheritage.com

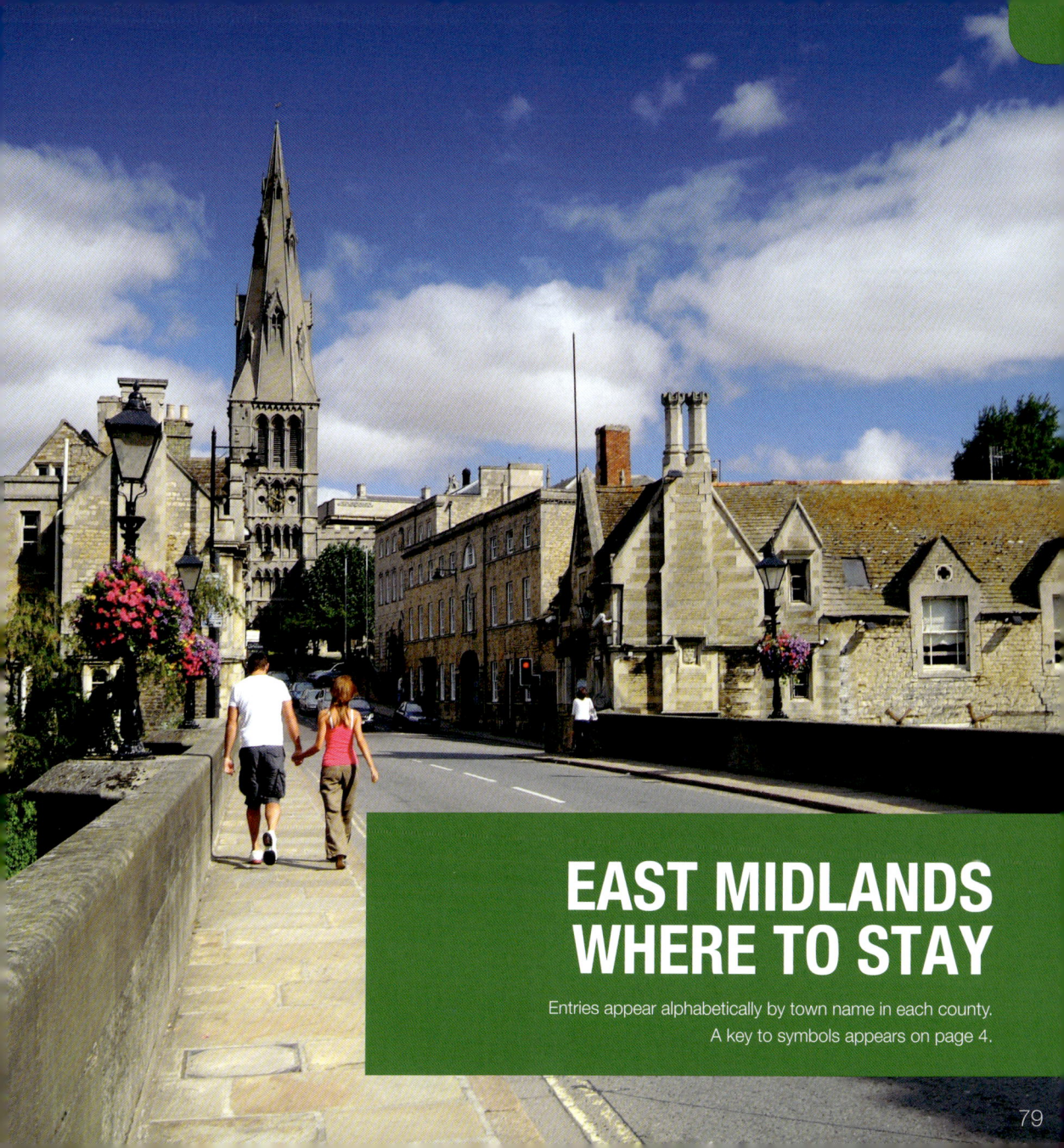

EAST MIDLANDS
WHERE TO STAY

Entries appear alphabetically by town name in each county.

A key to symbols appears on page 4.

THE CAVENDISH HOTEL

Church Lane, Baslow, Derbyshire DE45 1SP
T: (01246) 582311 **F:** (01246) 582312
E: info@cavendish-hotel.net **W:** www.cavendish-hotel.net

There has been an Inn here for so long that it is uncertain when it was built. Originally the Peacock Inn owned by the Duke of Rutland, it became the property of the Duke of Devonshire (and still is) in 1830. Becoming the Cavendish in the early 1970's it has been operated since 1975 by Eric Marsh, latterly with Philip Joseph under contract on behalf of Chatsworth Estates. A closely knit team is dedicated to looking after guests as individuals, not merely room numbers. The hotel exudes a quiet elegance, with extensive artworks and antiques and regular refurbishment work. The bathrooms have all been refurbished to a very high quality. The two AA Rosette (86%) awarded dining room is overseen by chef Mike Thompson. Added to this, all bedrooms have glorious views over Chatsworth Estate and the result is that elusive element - tranquillity.

DINING: Breakfast from 1000; dinner from £20.00.

BEDROOMS: 24
All bedrooms have glorious views over Chatsworth Estate.

B&B PER ROOM PER NIGHT:
S: £150.00 - £310.00
D: £195.00 - £310.00

ADDITIONAL INFORMATION:
Open all year.

Site: ❀ P **Payment:** 💷 € **Leisure:** ♪ ⋃ **Property:** ⛵ 📺 📖 🎪 ◑ ✿ **Children:** 🐕 🛏 ⚲
Catering: ⟨✕ ⛾ 🍴 **Room:** 📞 ✦ ☎ 🎧 📺 📀

LOSEHILL HOUSE HOTEL & SPA

BEDROOMS: 23
The beautifully furnished bedrooms, including family suites and deluxe kings, all have modern facilities, including flat screen TVs and DVD players. Most overlook the stunning surrounding countryside.

B&B PER ROOM PER NIGHT:
S: £165.00
D: £195.00

ADDITIONAL INFORMATION:
Spa Breaks from £300 lunch, dinner, b&b, two x 1 hour spa treatments. Easter & Christmas breaks also available. Sailing, caving and abseiling nearby.

Edale Road, Hope, Hope Valley, Derbyshire S33 6RF
T: (01433) 621219 **F:** (01433) 622501
E: info@losehillhouse.co.uk **W:** www.losehillhouse.co.uk

Losehill House is a unique country retreat in the Hope Valley in Derbyshire, where service and style are of the utmost importance. The hotel is furnished in modern style with common areas and passageways finished in solid oak. When we stayed, we were recommended a walk up Lose Hill which affords excellent views and is well signed. This worked up a good appetite for our delicious table d'hôte dinner, taken in the Orangery overlooking the valley. Hope Station, with its single track line, provides rail links to Sheffield and the north west. The hotel is available for exclusive wedding or function use. This is the very heart of the Peak District and the Pennine Way starts near the hotel. After a day's walking or sightseeing, why not curl up with a good book or take a dip in the indoor heated pool or the outdoor tub? The Spa treatment rooms offer a totally relaxing experience. Children are welcomed.

DINING: 2 AA Rosette restaurant. À la carte dinner £39.50; 7 Course Taster Menu £49.50; lunch & special diets available; last orders 2130 breakfast from 0730.

Site: ❀ P **Payment:** 💳 **Leisure:** ♪ ▶ ♉ ⚹ ⚘ 🏊 🦢 **Property:** 📶 ▤ 🖥 🏛 **Children:** 🧸 ▥
Catering: (✕ 🍷 🍽 **Room:** 📶 🧴 ☎ 📷

BIGGIN HALL HOTEL

Biggin by Hartington, Buxton, Derbyshire SK17 0DH
T: (01298) 84451
E: enquiries@bigginhall.co.uk **W:** www.bigginhall.co.uk

Biggin Hall is an historic old hall of 17th century origin, situated 1000 ft above sea level in the Peak District National Park. The Hall is Grade II* Listed and stands in its own grounds of some eight acres. Dinner is a daily changing menu of traditional home cooking with the emphasis on local ingredients and free range wholefoods. Guests have a choice of two sitting rooms and will feel very much at home in this exceptionally welcoming, comfortable house. Hosts James Moffett and Steven Williams will be able to recommend walking itineraries and traffic-free cycle trails. There are several historic houses nearby: Haddon Hall, Chatsworth and Kedleston Hall. Also close by are important archeological sites including Arkwrights Mill, Cromford Canal, Ecton Hill lead and copper mines and Magpie lead mine – Britain's deepest. Packed lunches can be arranged and there even is stabling if you wish to bring your horse or pony.

DINING: Dinner b&b from £130 per night for two (midweek low season) to £182 (weekend high season). Packed lunches available.

BEDROOMS: 21
There are eight bedrooms in the main house and a further 13 in converted buildings in the grounds: The Lodge, The Bothy and The Courtyard.

B&B PER ROOM PER NIGHT:
S: £80.00 - £100.00
D: £90.00 - £142.00

ADDITIONAL INFORMATION:
Double/twin room from £90 (apartments)/£106 main house & bothy. Double as single from £80. Seasonal specials – midweek from £130 per night, dinner, b&b including packed lunch and glühwein. Sorry – no children under 12.

Site: **P** Payment: 🔲 Leisure: ♿ 🎱 ☾ Property: 🚬 🐕

MANNERS ARMS

BEDROOMS: 10
The ten bedrooms are all individually and comfortably furnished. The largest ones are on the top floor and there are two good singles.

B&B PER ROOM PER NIGHT:
S: £70.00
D: £90.00

ADDITIONAL INFORMATION:
Sunday night offer double room £100 dinner, bed and breakfast.

Croxton Road, Knipton, Nr Grantham, Lincolnshire NG32 1PE
T: (01476) 879222
E: info@mannersarms.com **W:** www.mannersarms.com

The Manners Arms, formerly The Red House and originally a Hunting Lodge built for the 6th duke, has been thoughtfully restored to make a superior Restaurant with Rooms in the shadow of Belvoir Castle. The AA Rosette restaurant is a destination in its own right and attracts diners from a wide radius. Emphasis is on locally sourced modern British food. Starters include fresh crab or homemade terrines. Main courses might be heart of rump or fresh fish specials. There is a good wine list or four kinds of real ale to choose from in the bar, including one brewed in the Vale of Belvoir. Lighter bar menus are also available Monday to Saturday at lunch or supper time. These and breakfast can be enjoyed in the conservatory or in fine weather on the terrace. This area is also licensed for civil wedding ceremonies and civil partnerships. As well as Belvoir Castle, local attractions include Belton House, Denton Manor, and further afield, Burghley House and Rutland Water.

DINING: À la carte menu, plus bar food availbale; last orders 2100; breakfast from 0700.

Site: ✤ P Payment: 💷 Property: 🎣 🐕 📠 ⌀ Children: 🛝 🛏 ⚲ Catering: 🍴 ⚲ Room: 🍵 ⚲ 💿 📺

WASHINGBOROUGH HALL HOTEL

Church Hill, Washingborough, Lincoln, Lincolnshire LN4 1BE
T: (01522) 790340 **F:** (01522) 792936
E: enquiries@washingboroughhall.com **W:** www.washingboroughhall.com

A quintessential Georgian country house dating back to the early 1700s, the Hall is set in three acres of secluded grounds, just over two miles from Lincoln's historic city centre. Privately owned and managed by Edward and Lucy Herring, the Hall is a stylish, relaxed hotel renowned for its friendly atmosphere, great food and personal service. The elegant, yet informal dining room serves a seasonal British menu, using prime Lincolnshire ingredients where possible. A delicious Lincolnshire afternoon tea is available, and all day snacks and bar meals are served in the lounge bar. The hotel is perfect for weddings or special occasions and can cater for receptions for up to 120 people. Three well equipped function rooms can accommodate meetings and private parties. The Hall can also be hired on an exclusive use basis.

DINING: 2 AA Rosette Restaurant open every day. Booking essential.
Starters £5.50 - £8.50, mains £12.50 - £25.00, desserts £6.50.

BEDROOMS: 12
There are 12 individually designed bedrooms, including two four-posters. All retain the best of their original features, with the emphasis on comfort.

B&B PER ROOM PER NIGHT:
S: £85.00 - £122.50
D: £135.00 - £175.00

ADDITIONAL INFORMATION:
Open all year. Available for exclusive use family gatherings, corporate events and weddings. Well positioned for cycling excursions into Lincoln or onto the Sustrans Route One National Cycleway.

Site: ❀ **P Payment:** 🔲 **Leisure:** 🏌 **Property:** ♜ 🐾 🖥 ⌀ **Children:** 🛏 ⚲ **Catering:** (✕ 🍸 🍽 **Room:** 🔊 💧 📞 📺 📀 🛎

THE TALBOT HOTEL

BEDROOMS: 34
The 34 bedrooms are made up of standard, feature rooms and suites, some with four-posters and separate sitting areas. All are super comfortable with Beltrami linen, White Company toiletries and free internet access. Feature Room - £125 - £165. Suite - £135 - £195.

B&B PER ROOM PER NIGHT:
S: £75.00 - £95.00
D: £85.00 - £125.00

ADDITIONAL INFORMATION:
The hotel is fully licensed for weddings and is equipped with the latest in conference facilities.

New Street, Oundle, Northamptonshire PE8 4EA
T: (01832) 273621 **F:** (01832) 274545
E: talbot@bulldogmail.co.uk **W:** www.thetalbot-oundle.com

The Talbot Hotel, in the centre of the fine market town of Oundle, dates from Elizabethan times. The oak staircase was brought from nearby Fotheringay Castle, down which it is said that Mary, Queen of Scots descended on the way to her execution in 1587. The Bulldog Hotel Group has recently completed a major restoration and refurbishment project and one of the highlights is the new open plan Sun Room which extends into the old courtyard and is a great place to enjoy lunch or afternoon tea. Cuisine is traditional British, all freshly prepared and making use of local produce where possible, and has recently been awarded one AA Rosette. After dinner, relax in the main bar with open fireplaces. The company's Greensleep initiative means that, for every hotel room sold, a tree is planted, so you can sleep soundly in the knowledge that you are helping the environment!

DINING: À la carte menu starters from £5, mains from £10, desserts from £5.

Site: ⚜ P Payment: 💳 Leisure: ▸ Property: ⊛ ⛄ 🐾 🖼 📺 ◐ ✎ Children: 🍼 🛏 🎒 Catering: ⦅✕ 🍷
Room: 🍵 🌿 📺 📀 🖊 🧳

WHITTLEBURY HALL HOTEL AND SPA

Whittlebury Hall, Whittlebury, Northamptonshire NN12 8QH
T: (0845) 400 0001 **F:** (01327) 857867
E: reservations@whittleburyhall.co.uk **W:** www.whittleburyhall.co.uk

Whittlebury Hall is a modern Georgian-style building surrounded by parkland and golf courses. Inside rich furnishings and fabrics combine to create an impressive hotel. An aperitif can be taken in the Silverstone Bar before heading to either the informal Astons Restaurant or the fine dining AA Rosette Murrays at Whittlebury Hall. Bentleys, a third outlet, provides a pizza and pasta option. The award winning Day Spa has the very latest in health, fitness and beauty facilities. For the energetic there is an extensive Gymnasium, or there is the whirlpool spa set amongst Roman ruins, together with a steam room and sauna. A range of beauty treatments is on offer, from facials to massage, Heat and Ice Experiences and body wraps. Day Spa Packages and Spa Breaks are available to both residents and outside members. Adjacent to the hotel the independent Whittlebury Golf Course offers a choice of four 9-hole courses to challenge every level of handicap.

DINING: Astons, Bentleys, Murrays Restaurants; meals from £17.50; special diets available; last orders 2130; breakfast 0700.

BEDROOMS: 213
All bedrooms are spacious doubles with many modern touches and thoughtful extras. Suites come with whirlpool spa bath and double showers.

B&B PER ROOM PER NIGHT:
S: £129.00 - £159.00
D: £159.00 - £189.00

ADDITIONAL INFORMATION:
enjoyEngland.com 4 Star Hotel Silver Award 2014.

Site: ❀ P Payment: 💳 Leisure: ▶ ⚒ ⚊ Property: ♨ Catering: (✗ ⅄ Room: ☊ ✹ TV DVD

LANGAR HALL

BEDROOMS: 12

B&B PER ROOM PER NIGHT:
S: £95.00 - £140.00
D: £130.00 - £199.00

ADDITIONAL INFORMATION:
Sunday & Monday nights, dinner b&b from £150 per room per night. Newark antique fair. Trent Bridge cricket, Belvoir Castle, Belton House and Burghley House nearby.

Langar, Nottingham NG13 9HG
T: (01949) 860559 **F:** (01949) 861045
E: info@langarhall.co.uk **W:** www.langarhall.com

I always love my visits to Langar Hall. Although close to Nottingham, it is beautifully situated overlooking the Vale of Belvoir – a lovely country house, built in 1837, standing beside an early English church, with glorious views over the gardens and parkland. The Hall is the family home of Imogen Skirving, whose father used to entertain famous cricketers of the 1930's. Langar still attracts cricket lovers and famous old cricketers. The public rooms are delightful. The charming proprietor and her excellent team make every effort for their guests' happiness. Chef Gary Booth & his team work hard to produce excellent, reasonably priced menus of French and English food, using local produce, garden vegetables and herbs, Langar lamb, local stilton, game from the Belvoir estate, fish direct from Brixham. We had delicious seared scallops, followed by guinea fowl, then gooseberry pudding. All the bedrooms are charming and uniquely furnished. A truly lovely spot, with a peaceful and relaxing atmosphere.

DINING: 2 course AA table d'hôte dinner weekdays £25; à la carte menus from £35; lunch from £18.50; special diets available; last orders 2130; breakfast from 0700.

Site: ❀ **P Payment:** ⊞ € **Leisure:** ♪ ▶ **Property:** ♟ 🐾 🖼 🖥 🍴 ◐ ∅ **Children:** 🐕 🏠 🎠
Catering: (✗ 🍷 🍽 **Room:** 🌡 ☕ ☎

BARNSDALE LODGE HOTEL

The Avenue, Exton LE15 8AH
T: (01572) 724678 **F:** (01572) 724961
E: enquiries@barnsdalelodge.co.uk **W:** www.barnsdalelodge.co.uk

Overlooking Rutland Water and the undulating hills of England's smallest county, this former 17th century farm-house, adjacent to the estate of the Earl of Gainsborough, is an idyllic retreat for anyone wishing to escape. Lovingly restored, Barnsdale is north east of Oakham, with its market square and specialist boutiques and shops. Dining is in one of three dining rooms, the conservatory or, weather permitting, in the courtyard garden. All are usually full of local, contented diners. Eggs, herbs and vegetables come from the hotel's own hens and vegetable garden. There is a Meadow Walk (for dogs) and Highland cattle to observe. Conferences, wedding receptions, product launches and private parties take place in the separate Banqueting Suite. Vicienté at Barnsdale, the hotel's beauty therapy room and the adjoining William Wheelwright hair salon offer the ultimate in relaxation and pampering.

DINING: AA Rosette dinner table d'hôte 3 course from £28.50; à la carte, lunch & special diets available; last orders 2130; breakfast from 0700.

BEDROOMS: 45
Bedrooms offer complete relaxation. Two are specially designed for disabled guests, some are inter-connecting or four-poster and many offer views towards Rutland Water.

B&B PER ROOM PER NIGHT:
S: £80.00 - £95.00
D: £95.00 - £150.00

ADDITIONAL INFORMATION:
Stay three nights and receive free entrance into Geoff Hamilton's famous Barnsdale Gardens. Rates from £325.50. Please ask for details.

Retreats are 3 nights from £365 and 7 from £495. Open all year.

Site: ✿ P **Payment:** 🏧 **Leisure:** ▸ ☉ ⚒ **Property:** ⚓ 🐎 🚲 **Catering:** ❨✗ 🍷 🍴 **Room:** ✎ 🚰 ☎ 📺 🗄

HEART OF ENGLAND
Herefordshire, Shropshire, Staffordshire, Warwickshire, West Midlands, Worcestershire

The Heart of England: a name that defines this lovely part of the country so much better than its geographical name: The Midlands. Like a heart it has many arteries and compartments, from the March counties of Shropshire and Herefordshire, through Birmingham and the West Midlands, birthplace of the Industrial Revolution. It is a region rich in history and character and you'll find pretty villages, grand castles and plenty of canals and waterways to explore.

HEART OF ENGLAND

COVENTRY & WARWICKSHIRE

From castles and cathedrals to art galleries, museums and exciting events, this region captivates visitors from all over the world. A beautifully preserved Tudor town on the banks of the Avon and Warwickshire's most visited, Stratford-upon-Avon is the bard's birthplace with numerous theatres playing Shakespeare and other dramatists' work.

Warwick Castle
Warwickshire CV34 4QU
0871 265 2000
www.warwick-castle.co.uk
Battlements, towers, turrets, History, magic, myth and adventure - Warwick Castle is a Scheduled Ancient Monument and Grade 1 listed building packed with things to do, inside and out.

The city of Warwick is dominated by its 14th century castle and its museums, and plenty of family activities are staged throughout the year. Historic Coventry has over 400 listed buildings and is most famous for its cathedrals, with the modern Church of St Michael sitting majestically next to the 'blitzed' ruins of its 14th century predecessor.

HEREFORDSHIRE

Herefordshire's ruined castles in the border country and Iron Age and Roman hill-forts recall a turbulent battle-scarred past. Today the landscape is peaceful, with delightful small towns and villages and Hereford cattle grazing in pastures beside apple orchards and hop gardens. Fine historic houses and castles include elegant Eastnor Castle at Ledbury, while Kington is home to the charming Hergest Croft Gardens.

Hereford has an 11th century cathedral and the Mappa Mundi while in the west, the Wye meanders through meadows and valleys. Hay-on-Wye is now best known for its annual Book Festival and plethora of second hand bookshops.

Hereford Cathedral
Herefordshire HR1 2NG
(01432) 374202
www.herefordcathedral.org
Some of the finest examples of architecture from Norman times to the present day.

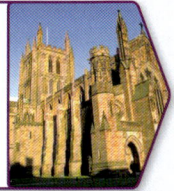

SHROPSHIRE

Tucked away on the England/Wales border, Shropshire is another March county that saw much conflict between English and Welsh, hostilities between warring tribes and invading Romans.

The Wrekin and Stretton Hills were created by volcanoes and in the south the Long Mynd rises to 1700 ft with panoramic views of much of the Severn plain. Ironbridge, near the present day Telford, is said to be where the Industrial Revolution started in Britain. County town Shrewsbury was an historic fortress town built in a loop of the river Severn and the birthplace of Charles Darwin. These days it joins Ludlow, with its 11th century castle, as one of the gastronomic high spots of Britain.

Iron Bridge and Toll House
Telford, Shropshire TF8 7DG
(01952) 433424
www.ironbridge.org.uk
The Ironbridge Gorge is a remarkable and beautiful insight into the region's industrial heritage. Ten award-winning Museums spread along the valley beside the wild River Severn - still spanned by the world's first Iron Bridge.

STAFFORDSHIRE

Staffordshire, squeezed between the Black Country to the south and Manchester to the north, is home to the Potteries, a union of six towns made famous by Wedgwood, Spode and other ceramic designers. Lichfield has a magnificent three-spired 13th century cathedral and was birthplace of Samuel Johnson.

The unspoilt ancient heathland of Cannock Chase, leafy woodlands of the National Forest and secluded byways of South Staffordshire all offer the chance to enjoy the great outdoors.

WEST MIDLANDS

The West Midlands is an urban area, criss-crossed by motorways, and still represents the powerhouse of Central Britain. Historically Birmingham's prosperity was based on factories, hundreds of small workshops and a network of canals, all of which helped in the production of everything from needles and chocolate to steam engines and bridges. Nowadays the city has one of the best concert halls in Europe, excellent shopping and a regenerated waterside café culture.

Affluent Sutton Coldfield and Solihull have proud civic traditions and a number of pretty parks including Sutton Park and Brueton Park. Many of Solihull's rural villages sit along the Stratford-upon-Avon canal and offer plenty of picturesque pubs along the tow path from which to watch the gentle meander of passing narrow boats.

Wolverhampton has been called Capital of the Black Country, made famous through its ironwork and Walsall, birthplace of Jerome K Jerome, has three museums.

Birmingham Botanical Gardens
West Midlands B15 3TR
(0121) 454 1860
www.birminghambotanicalgardens.org.uk
Visit the 15 acres of ornamental gardens and glasshouses at Birmingham Botanical Gardens and Glasshouses in Edgbaston.

WORCESTERSHIRE

The beautiful county of Worcestershire has a fantastic selection of historic houses and gardens to discover and Worcester itself has a famous cathedral, cricket ground, and 15th century Commandery, now a Civil war museum.

Great Malvern, still a Spa town, is famous as the birthplace of Sir Edward Elgar, who drew much of his inspiration from this countryside and who is celebrated at the annual Malvern Festival. The old riverside market town of Evesham is the centre of the Vale of Evesham fruit and vegetable growing area which, with the tranquil banks of the river Avon and the undulating hills and peaceful wooded slopes of the Cotswolds, offers some of the prettiest landscapes in the country.

Droitwich, known in Roman times as Salinae, still has briny water in its spa baths and can trace the origins of salt extraction in the area back to prehistoric times, it even holds an annual Salt Festival to celebrate this unique heritage.

HUDSON'S HISTORIC HOUSES & GARDENS HIGHLIGHTS

Arbury Hall
(024) 7638 2804
www.arburyestate.co.uk
The 'Gothic Gem' of the Midlands. The principal rooms stand as a breathtaking example of early gothic revival architecture.

Charlecote Park
(01789) 470277
www.nationaltrust.org.uk
A picture of peace and repose. The house holds surprising treasures and the gardens present a riot of colour.

Chillington Hall
(01902) 580236
www.chillingtonhall.co.uk
18th Century house completed by John Soane with 'Capability' Brown parkland laid out in the 1760s.

Compton Verney
(01926) 645500
www.competonverney.org.uk
A unique art gallery experience set within a Grade 1 listed mansion remodelled by Robert Adams in the 1760s.

Croome
(01905) 371006
www.nationaltrust.org.uk
The landscaped parkland at Croome is a masterpiece in landscape design and boasts the title of 'Capability' Brown's first.

Eastnor Castle
(01531) 633160
www.eastnorcastle.com
Inside, the castle boasts a 60 ft high hall and state rooms including the Pugin Gothic Drawing Room.

Harvington Hall
(01562) 777846
www.harvingtonhall.com
A moated medieval and Elizabethan manor house containing the finest series of priest hides in the country.

Upton Cressett Hall
(01746) 714616
www.uptoncressetthall.co.uk
Moated, romantic Grade 1 Elizabethan Manor with magnificent gatehouse and Norman Church.

Weston Park
(01952) 852100
www.weston-park.com
This magnificent house boasts internationally important patintings, furniture and objets d'art plus 1000 acres of glorious Parkland.

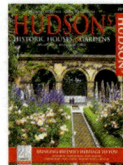

HUDSON'S HISTORIC HOUSES & GARDENS
MUSEUMS & HERITAGE SITES

For more suggestions of great historic days out across Britain visit
www.hudsonsheritage.com

HEART OF ENGLAND
WHERE TO STAY

Entries appear alphabetically by town name in each county.
A key to symbols appears on page 4.

CASTLE HOUSE

Castle Street, Hereford, Herefordshire HR1 2NW
T: (01432) 356321 **F:** (01432) 365909
E: info@castlehse.co.uk **W:** www.castlehse.co.uk

Castle House is an elegant Grade II listed Georgian villa just yards from the historic cathedral, in the city of Hereford. In the main hotel, the decor is bold, with tapestries, paintings and filled with fresh flowers while the rooms in Number 25, a separate townhouse just yards from the main building, are more contemporary. There are two ground floor suites, one of which is fully equipped for those with special needs and the other has its own terrace leading out into the hotel's garden which overlooks the old castle moat. Having been the old capital of Mercia, Hereford is steeped in history. The cathedral's famous Mappa Mundi, Chained Library and signed Magna Carta are within walking distance, as are the main shops and new the shopping complex. Award-winning head chef Claire Nicholls creates memorable lunch and dinner menus, including a seven-course Tasting Menu, in the restaurant and in the Castle Bar and Bistro, offering the best of contemporary British cuisine using local ingredients, some from the owner's nearby farm.

DINING: 2 AA Rosette restaurant. 3 course dinner in Ballingham Bar & Bistro from £22; Taste of Marches 7 course table d'hôte.

Site: ✿ P **Payment:** 🖃 € **Leisure:** ♪ **Property:** ⊛ ⛺ 🚽 🗄 🏥 ◐ **Children:** 🐾 🛏 🎢
Catering: (✕ ☕ 🍽 **Room:** 🔧 💧 📞 🎮 📺 📠 🔌 🗄

BEDROOMS: 24
Individually designed luxury rooms and suites, Every bedroom has flatscreen TV/DVD, Wi-Fi, a selection of teas and coffee, a fridge with fresh milk and a welcoming decanter of sherry. Bathrooms all en suite and decorated with marble and wood.

B&B PER ROOM PER NIGHT:
S: £130.00
D: £150.00 - £230.00

ADDITIONAL INFORMATION:
Open all year.

AA
★★★
Hotel

THE CHASE HOTEL

BEDROOMS: 38
Bedrooms all have voicemail telephones, modem points, Wi-Fi Internet access as well as the usual amenities. Executive and four-poster rooms enjoy the extra comfort of a feature or jacuzzi bathroom.

B&B PER ROOM PER NIGHT:
S: £59.00 - £190.00
D: £69.00 - £210.00

ADDITIONAL INFORMATION:
Open all year.

Gloucester Road, Ross-on-Wye, Herefordshire HR9 5LH
T: (01989) 763161 **F:** (01989) 768330
E: gm@chasehotel.co.uk **W:** www.chasehotel.co.uk

The Chase Hotel is a stately mansion set in 11 acres of parkland on the outskirts of Ross-on-Wye providing a smart 38-room country hotel. A large newly constructed outdoor patio area overlooking the grounds with ample seating is a great added feature and sure to be enjoyed by guests. Harry's Restaurant & Chase Lounge serve a fusion of dishes across one menu to a one AA Rosette standard. A typical starter might be double-baked Hereford hop cheese soufflé, followed maybe by roasted sea bass fillet with a mussel and saffron paella and rustic red wine sauce. Traditional Sunday lunch and a good selection of bar snacks are also available. Weddings, conferences and special events can be organised. The hotel can also arrange hot air balloon flights, canoe trips down the river Wye and team building activities. Good walks start from the hotel, through picturesque Ross and along the river towpaths. It is well placed for exploring Welsh border country and historic castles and gardens in the area.

DINING: 3 course à la carte from £27.50; lunch, special diets available; last orders 2200; breakfast from 0700.

Site: ❀ **P Payment:** 💳 € **Leisure:** ► **Property:** 🏆 🖥 🗄 ♫ ◐ **Children:** 🛏 🍴 ♿ **Catering:** 🍴✗ 🍷 🍽
Room: 🔌 ✆ 📺 📀 🎛

MYTTON & MERMAID HOTEL

Atcham, Shrewsbury SY5 6QG
T: (01743) 761220 **F:** (01743) 761292
E: reception@myttonandmermaid.co.uk **W:** www.myttonandmermaid.co.uk

A fine, family owned country house hotel on the banks of the river Severn, three miles from Shrewsbury town centre. It has the charm of an old coaching inn, having stood on the old A5 London-Holyhead route. In the 1930s, it was bought by Sir Clough Williams Ellis of Portmeirion and Romney Bay House fame. It was extended and converted into a hotel, assuming the name Mytton & Mermaid, the mermaid being the crest of Portmeirion. Today it guards the old Atcham Bridge and enjoys lovely views and sweeping river lawns. The hotel offers mini breaks, and the Mytton Sunday break is very popular. The heart of the hotel is the AA two Rosette Restaurant, which uses Shropshire local produce where possible, with menus changing to reflect the seasons. Afternoon tea with homemade cakes has become very popular.

DINING: AA 2 Rosette Restaurant. Food 0700 until 2200 and includes childrens' and vegetarian or vegan menus. Picnic hampers. 3 course table d'hôte dinner £25pp; Seasonal à la carte menu; Last orders 2200; breakfast from 0715 Mon-Fri & from 0800 Sat-Sun.

BEDROOMS: 18
The 18 bedrooms range from the Mytton four-poster through to the Courtyard rooms, which are very popular. Nice touches within the bedrooms include homemade flapjacks and a wide range of coffee and teas.

B&B PER ROOM PER NIGHT:
S: £50.00 - £95.00
D: £90.00 - £110.00

ADDITIONAL INFORMATION:
Open all year. The hotel also owns the quaint oak-beamed Bramble Cottage opposite nearby National Trust Attingham Park, a self-contained alternative for up to six people.

Site: ❀ P **Payment:** 🖃 **Leisure:** ⚲ ∪ **Property:** ♟ 🏇 🗐 ♨ ◑ **Children:** ⌇ **Catering:** (✗ ⍭ 🍴
Room: 🗠 ♨ ☎ 📺

SOULTON HALL

BEDROOMS: 8

Rooms in Soulton Hall boast wood panelling and mullion windows whilst further ground floor accommodation is available in the Carriage House and Cedar House. The bedrooms are sumptuous and lovingly decorated with fine fabrics and generous, comfortable beds.

B&B PER ROOM PER NIGHT:
S: £52.00 - £149.00
D: £104.00 - £164.00

ADDITIONAL INFORMATION:
Open all year.

Soulton Road, Wem, Shropshire SY4 5RS
T: (01939) 232786 **F:** (01939) 234097
E: enquiries@soultonhall.co.uk **W:** www.soultonhall.co.uk/page/286/book.htm

16 generations of the Ashton family have cherished this ancient Shropshire manor house, set in 500 acres of private country estate and woodland as John and Ann Ashton, and son Tim do today. Guests here are treated like members of the family. Drinks are taken in the cosy drawing room, whilst making a choice from the four-course menu. This is served in the elegant candle-lit dining room, using local ingredients including game from the estate and fruit from the garden. The 18th century Soulton Court (across the lawn) also now provides a unique setting for weddings and conferences. Soulton, with its walled gardens and extensive grounds, is a peaceful spot in which to just relax. It is a working farm and also an excellent base from which to explore the beauties of the Shires and the Welsh Marches, as well as the Ironbridge Gorge and the cities of Shrewsbury and Chester. The Welsh Hills and border castles are also within easy reach. Soulton is one of the best kept secrets of Shropshire.

DINING: 4 course table d'hôte dinner £38.50 – 42; special diets available; last orders 2030.

AA
★★★★
Guest House

Site: ✿ P Payment: 💳 Property: ⚓ 🏠 Catering: (✕ 🍴 Room: 🔌 ✋ 📺 📀

COTTAGE IN THE WOOD

Holywell Road, Malvern Wells, Malvern, Worcestershire WR14 4LG
T: (01684) 588860 **F:** (01684) 560662
E: reception@cottageinthewood.co.uk **W:** www.cottageinthewood.co.uk

High above the village of Malvern Wells, half hidden amongst hillside trees, you will find this former Georgian dower house, now a hotel of charm and character run by John and Sue Pattin and family. Son and head chef Dominic presides in the two AA Rosette Outlook restaurant, which enjoys a 30 mile panoramic view across to the Cotswold Hills. Cuisine is modern English, making use of local suppliers wherever possible and complemented by a 500-bin wine list. Within the grounds are Beech Cottage, with four cottagey bedrooms, and The Pinnacles with 19 bedrooms, two with balconies and six with patio seating areas. If you can be persuaded to leave the soothing comfort of the rooms (many front facing), you can walk directly from the grounds onto the Malvern Hills. By car the area from the Welsh Marches to Shakespeare's Stratford awaits you, whilst all around is Elgar country, from which the great composer drew much of his inspiration.

DINING: The restaurant is à la carte with special diets catered for by prior arrangement. Dinner last orders 2045 and breakfast from 0730.

BEDROOMS: 30
All bedrooms are comfortably furnished and have tower air circulators, hospitality trays with tea/coffee and home made biscuits, useful room information folders and local mineral water. Bathrooms come with Duck toiletries, flannels etc.

B&B PER ROOM PER NIGHT:
S: £79.00 - £121.00
D: £99.00 - £198.00

ADDITIONAL INFORMATION:
Open all year. Dogs are welcome on the ground floor in the Pinnacles rooms. The Three Counties Showground lies just below the hotel.

AA ★★★ Hotel

Site: ❀ P Payment: 💷 Leisure: ▶ ∪ Property: 🐕 🐎 🖥 🎱 ⌀ Children: 🛏 🍴 ⚲ Catering: 🍽 🍷 🍴
Room: 🍵 ✆ 📺 📀

ECKINGTON MANOR

BEDROOMS: 17
Boutique bedrooms are furnished with silk wallpapers, designer furniture, carefully chosen light fittings and large comfortable beds dressed in the finest Italian cotton bed linen. Soft fluffy towels and The White Company toiletries await our guests in their own bespoke Fired Earth bathroom. Antler chandeliers, original exposed beams and brickwork and restored antiques.

B&B PER ROOM PER NIGHT:
S: £99.00 - £249.00
D: £129.00 - £249.00

ADDITIONAL INFORMATION:
Open all year.

Hammock Road, Eckington, Nr. Pershore, Worcestershire WR10 3BJ
T: (01386) 751600
E: info@eckingtonmanor.co.uk **W:** www.eckingtonmanor.co.uk

In 2004, Judy Gardner bought the run down Manor Farm in Eckington. She lovingly restored the farm and its buildings, diversifying to offer outstanding accommodation, where her eye for design and attention to detail has resulted in simply stunning bedrooms and suites; and a cookery school offering a plethora of courses teaching everything from basic knife skills to advanced courses. The lovingly restored accommodation has been awarded the highest accolade by VisitEngland – Gold. Individually designed rooms offer our guests laid back luxury, every detail has been carefully researched and chosen so that guests have a most comfortable and enjoyable stay. The Restaurant at Eckington Manor uses the very best available seasonal British ingredients. Responsibly sourced and featuring beef from our own farm, our chefs create British dishes with a European influence. From our Siberian goose down pillows to our award winning breakfast sausage, you can expect personal treatment from the caring and friendly team.

DINING: Lunch served 1130 - 1430. Dinner served 1900 - 2100, Tues - Sat inclusive; 3 courses from £38.00 per guest.

Site: ✿ P Payment: 💳 Property: ⬇ 🛏 🎱 Children: ⛷ Catering: ⦅✕ ☟ 🍴 Room: 🔌 ♨ 📺 📀 🔌

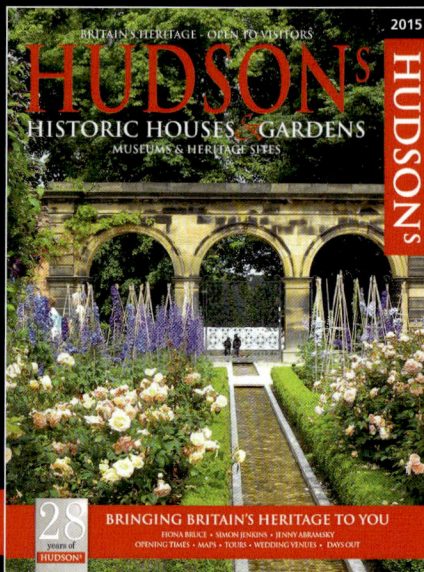

Yorkshire

YORKSHIRE

Yorkshire, the largest county in England, is one of the most popular and boasts award-winning culture, heritage and scenery. There's cosmopolitan Leeds, stylish Harrogate and rural market towns full of charm and character. The wild moors and deserted dales of the Yorkshire Dales and North York Moors National Parks are majestic in their beauty and the county has a spectacular coastline of rugged cliffs and sandy beaches. The region also has a wealth of historic houses, ruined castles, abbeys and fortresses for visitors to discover.

YORKSHIRE

NORTH YORKSHIRE

Steeped in history, North Yorkshire boasts some of the country's most splendid scenery. Wherever you go in The Dales, you'll be faced with breathtaking views and constant reminders of a historic and changing past. In medieval days, solid fortresses like Richmond and Middleham were built to protect the area from marauding Scots. Ripley and Skipton also had their massive strongholds, while Bolton Castle in Wensleydale once imprisoned Mary, Queen of Scots. The pattern of history continues with the great abbeys, like Jervaulx Abbey, near Masham, where the monks first made Wensleydale cheese and the majestic ruins of Fountains Abbey in the grounds of Studley Royal. Between the Dales and the North York Moors, Herriot Country is named for one of the world's best loved writers, James Herriot, who made the area his home for more than 50 years and whose books have enthralled readers with tales of Yorkshire life.

Castle Howard
Malton, North Yorkshire YO60 7DA
(01653) 648444
castlehoward.co.uk
A magnificent 18th century house situated in breathtaking parkland. Inside the House guides share stories of the house, family and collections, while outdoor-guided tours reveal the secrets of the architecture and landscape.

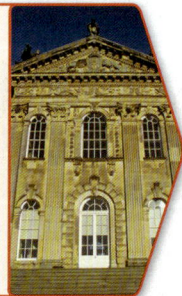

Escape to the wild, deserted North York Moors National Park with its 500 square miles of hills, dales, forests and open moorland, neatly edged by a spectacular coastline. Walking, cycling and pony trekking are ideal ways to savour the scenery and there are plenty of greystone towns and villages dotted throughout the Moors that provide ideal bases from which to explore. From Helmsley, visit the ruins of Rievaulx Abbey, founded by Cistercian monks in the 12th century or discover moorland life in the Ryedale Folk Museum at Hutton-le-Hole. The Beck Isle Museum in Pickering provides an insight into the life of a country market town and just a few miles down the road you'll find Malton, once a Roman fortress, and nearby Scampston Hall and Walled Garden.

YORK

Wherever you turn within the city's medieval walls, you will find glimpses of the past. The splendours of the 600-year old Minster, the grim stronghold of Clifford's Tower, the National Railway Museum, the medieval timbers of the Merchant Adventurers' Hall and the fascinating Jorvik Viking Centre all offer an insight into the history of this charming city. Throughout the city, statues and monuments remind the visitor that this was where Constantine was proclaimed Holy Roman Emperor, Guy Fawkes was born and Dick Turpin met his end.

Modern York is has excellent shopping, a relaxed cafe culture, first class restaurants and bars, museums, tours and attractions. Whether you visit for a romantic weekend or a fun-filled family holiday, there really is something for everyone.

York Minster
York, North Yorkshire YO1 7JN
(0)1904 557200
www.yorkminster.org
Regularly voted one of the most popular things to do in York, the Minster is not only an architecturally stunning building but is a place to discover the history of York over the centuries, its artefacts and treasures.

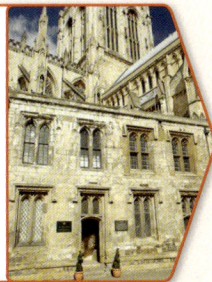

LEEDS & WEST YORKSHIRE

For centuries cloth has been spun from the wool of the sheep grazing in the Pennine uplands and the fascinating story of this industrial heritage can be seen in the numerous craft centres and folk museums throughout West Yorkshire. To enjoy the countryside, take a trip on the steam hauled Keighley and Worth Valley Railway. Not far from Haworth, home of the Brontë sisters, is Bingley, where the Leeds & Liverpool canal makes its famous uphill journey. Leeds itself is a vibrant city with its Victorian shopping arcades, Royal Armouries Museum and lively arts scene.

YORKSHIRE COASTLINE

The Yorkshire coastline is one of the UK's most naturally beautiful and rugged, where pretty fishing villages cling to rocky cliffs, in turn towering over spectacular beaches and family-friendly seaside destinations. At the northern end of the coastline, Saltburn is a sand and shingle beach popular with surfers and visitors can ride the Victorian tram from the cliff to the promenade during the summer. Whitby is full of quaint streets and bestowed with a certain Gothic charm. At Scarborough, one of Britain's oldest seaside resorts, the award-winning North Bay and South Bay sand beaches are broken by the rocky headland, home to the historic Scarborough Castle. Filey, with its endless sands, has spectacular views and a 40-mile stretch of perfect sandy beach sweeps south from the dramatic 400 ft high cliffs at Flamborough Head. Along this coastline you can find the boisterous holiday destination of Bridlington, or a gentler pace at pretty Hornsea and Withernsea.

Harewood House
Leeds, West Yorkshire LS17 9LG
(0113) 218 1010 • www.harewood.org
Harewood House, Bird Garden, Grounds and Adventure Playground - The Ideal day out for all the family.

EAST YORKSHIRE

From cosmopolitan Hull to the hills and valleys of the Yorkshire Wolds, East Yorkshire is wonderfully diverse. A landscape of swirling grasslands, medieval towns, manor houses and Bronze Age ruins contrasting with the vibrant energy and heritage of the Humber. The Wolds are only a stones throw from some great seaside resorts and Beverley, with its magnificent 13th century minster and lattice of medieval streets, is just one of the many jewels of architectural heritage to be found here. Hull is a modern city rebuilt since the war, linked to Lincolnshire via the impressive 1452 yd Humber Bridge.

Sheffield Botanical Gardens
South Yorkshire S10 2LN
(0114) 268 6001 · www.sbg.org.uk
Extensive gardens with over 5,500 species of plants, Grade II Listed garden pavillion.

SOUTH YORKSHIRE

The historic market town of Doncaster was founded by the Romans and has a rich horseracing and railway heritage. The area around Sheffield - the steel city - was once dominated by the iron and steel industries and was the first city in England to pioneer free public transport. The Industrial Museum and City Museum display a wide range of Sheffield cutlery and oplate. Today, Meadowhall shopping centre, with 270 stores under one roof, caters for avid shoppers.

HUDSON'S HISTORIC HOUSES & GARDENS HIGHLIGHTS

Burton Agnes Hall & Gardens
(01262) 490324
www.burtonagnes.com

A magnificent Elizabethan Hall containing treasures collected over four centuries, from the original carving and plasterwork to modern and impressionist paintings.

Duncombe Park
(01439) 770213
www.duncombepark.com

Historian Christopher Hussey describes the Park as *'the most spectacularly beautiful among English landscape conceptions of the 18th Century'*.

Fountains Abbey & Studley Royal
(01765) 608888
www.nationaltrust.org.uk

Spectacular ruin of a 12th Century Cisterian abbey. One of the best surviving examples of a Georgian water garden.

Kiplin Hall
(01748) 818178
www.kiplinhall.co.uk

Award-winning historic house and garden. Eclectic mix of previous owners' furniture, paintings, portraits and personalia.

Markenfield Hall
(01765) 692303
www.markenfield.com

"*This wonderfully little-altered building is the most complete example of the medium-sized 14th century country house in England*" John Martin Robinson, The Architecture of Northern England.

Newby Hall & Gardens
(01423) 322583
www.newbyhall.com

Its beautifully restored interior presents Robert Adam at his best. It houses rare Gobelins tapestries and one of the UK's largest private collections of classical statuary.

Nunnington Hall
(01439) 748283
www.nationaltrust.org.uk

Picturesque Yorkshire Manor house wth organic garden and exciting exhibitions.

Skipton Castle
(01756) 792442
www.skiptoncastle.co.uk

Skipton Castle, over 900 years old, one of the best preserved, most complete medieval castles in England.

Wassand Hall
(01964) 534488
www.wassand.co.uk

Fine Regency house from 1815. Beautifully restored walled gardens, woodlands walks, Parks and vistas.

HUDSON'S
HISTORIC HOUSES & GARDENS
MUSEUMS & HERITAGE SITES

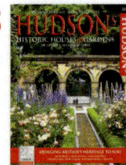

For more suggestions of great historic days out across Britain visit
www.hudsonsheritage.com

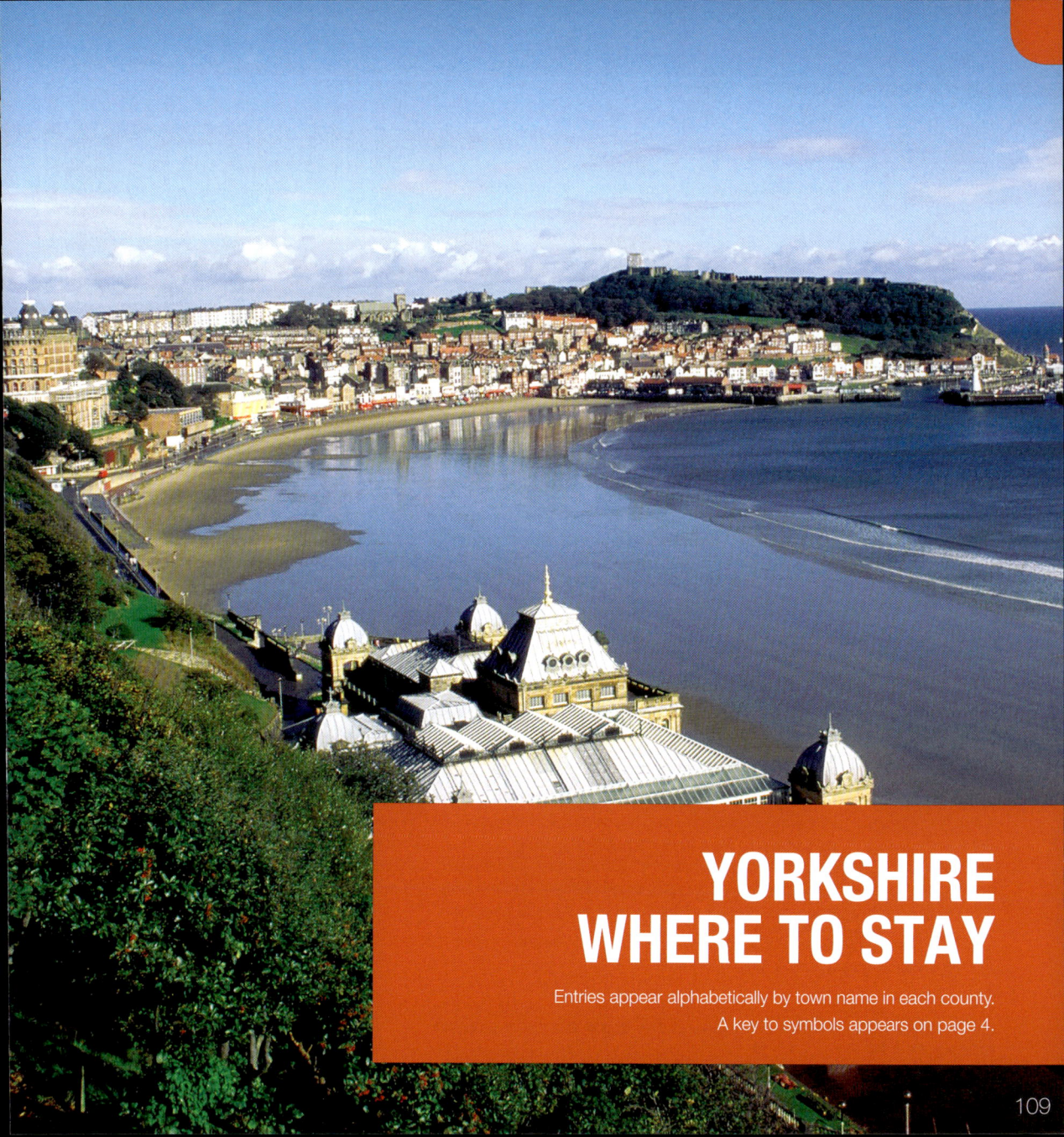

YORKSHIRE
WHERE TO STAY

Entries appear alphabetically by town name in each county.
A key to symbols appears on page 4.

THE FEVERSHAM ARMS HOTEL & VERBENA SPA

High Street, Helmsley, North Yorkshire YO62 5AG
T: (01439) 770766 **F:** (01439) 770346
E: info@fevershamarmshotel.com **W:** www.fevershamarmshotel.com

This secluded luxury retreat lies in the heart of Helmsley in North Yorkshire. Surrounded by countryside, our award-winning hotel and spa is hidden away so you can relax, unwind and indulge. Cosy yet contemporary and with artwork to rival a gallery. Outdoors the hotel boasts a unique Mediterranean terrace and outdoor pool while indoors open fires and snugs make our guests feel welcome all year round. The sky lit restaurant is sumptuously decorated in a warm and elegant colour palette designed to be welcoming all year round. The modern British menu draws heavily upon our local landscape regularly featuring rich Yorkshire game and fresh North Sea fish and seafood, with two AA rosettes the restaurant is renowned for both its à la carte and signature tasting menus. To complement the food there is a well-stocked cellar and an extensive selection of after dinner wines and liqueurs.

DINING: Seasonal market menu £48 pp, à la carte items individually priced, Six Course Tasting Menu £60 pp.

BEDROOMS: 33
5 Standard, 8 Executive, 3 Junior Suite, 9 Deluxe Suite, 4 Poolside Suite, 4 Spa Suite.

B&B PER ROOM PER NIGHT:
S: £110.00 - £265.00
D: £120.00 - £430.00

ADDITIONAL INFORMATION:
Open all year.

Site: P Payment: 🔲 **Leisure:** 🔳 ♨ ⚘ **Property:** 🔺 🐾 🔲 🔲 🔲 ◑ ⊘ **Children:** 🔲 🔲 🔺
Catering: 🔲 🔲 🔲 **Room:** 🔲 🔲 🔲 🔲

SPORTSMANS ARMS HOTEL & RESTAURANT

BEDROOMS: 11
9 Doubles, 2 twins, all en suite. 4 ground floor rooms available.

B&B PER ROOM PER NIGHT:
S: £90.00 - £100.00
D: £120.00 - £130.00

ADDITIONAL INFORMATION:
End October – mid March Nidderdale Midweekers – 2 persons sharing, min stay two nights, dinner, b&b from £170 per person Sun – Thurs inc.

In The Times 2015 Top 25 Sunday lunch venues.

Wath-in-Nidderdale, Pateley Bridge, North Yorkshire HG3 5PP
T: (01423) 711306 **F:** (01423) 712524
E: sportsmansarms@btconnect.com **W:** www.sportsmans-arms.co.uk

The Sportsman's Arms Hotel and Restaurant nestles close to the river Nidd (on which it has fishing rights) at Wath in Nidderdale - a conservation village, and one of the most picturesque and unspoiled villages in a beautiful part of the Yorkshire Dales. Reached by a pack horse bridge and set in its own gardens, this attractive 17th century mellow sandstone building attracts you like a magnet. Ray and Jane Carter and their family have been welcoming guests to The Sportsman's Arms hotel and restaurant for thirty six years now. Throughout this time their aims have been simple - to create a relaxed and unpretentious atmosphere and to offer experiences that will encourage diners and guests to return again and again. The restaurant features only fresh, local produce and superb seafood. Comfortable bedrooms with traditional fabrics, individually furnished, en suite with Molton Brown toiletries. Winner of the National Countryside Alliance Locals to Locals Honest Food Competition.

DINING: À la carte dinner £30 - £50. Bar food available; special diets available; dinner from 1900 – 2100.

Site: ❀ P **Payment:** 💳 **Leisure:** ♪ ⚒ **Property:** 🐾 ▦ ♨ ⌀ **Children:** ➤ **Catering:** ⟨✗ ⟐ 🍽 **Room:** 🗑 ☂ 📞 🖐

LASTINGHAM GRANGE COUNTRY HOUSE HOTEL

High Street, Lastingham, North Yorkshire YO62 6TH
T: (01751) 417345 **F:** (01751) 417358
E: reservations@lastinghamgrange.com **W:** www.lastinghamgrange.com

It is easy to see why guests return time and again to this charming hotel situated on the edge of the Moors in the historic village of Lastingham, a peaceful backwater in the heart of the North York Moors National Park. The old, stone-walled country house, built around a courtyard and set within 10 acres of attractive gardens, is owned and personally run by the Wood family. Their charming friendliness and hospitality sets the mood for all guests to feel at ease in this elegant and tasteful country home. The atmosphere is unhurried and peaceful, the south facing terrace providing a tranquil setting in which to relax and enjoy the beautiful rose garden. The welcoming hall, the spacious lounge with its open fire, the comfortable bedrooms with their impressive views, the excellent food, the attention to detail and the location make the Grange a perfect spot for a restful break. In the village is the 7th century Church of St Mary with its ancient crypt, mentioned by the Venerable Bede in AD 731 and where Holy Communion is still celebrated every Wednesday morning.

DINING: Table d'hôte dinner £39.50; lunch from £20; Sunday lunch from £29.50; special diets available; last orders 2030.

Site: ✿ P **Payment:** £3 € **Leisure:** ♪ ⏵ ∪ **Property:** ⌂ ⊞ ⊡ ⋈ ⊘ **Children:** ⥤ ⊞ ⚲
Catering: (✗ ⚒ ⚒ **Room:** ⌇ ⚲ ☏ ⊡

BEDROOMS: 11

B&B PER ROOM PER NIGHT:
S: £135.00 - £140.00
D: £199.00

ADDITIONAL INFORMATION:
2 nights, dinner, B&B, two sharing, £265 per room per night. Also see website.

AA
★★★
Hotel

THE CONISTON HOTEL

BEDROOMS: 71
The bedrooms are all very comfortable, with all having excellent views, some with external balconies and sitting areas.

B&B PER ROOM PER NIGHT:
S: £90.00
D: £99.00

ADDITIONAL INFORMATION:
Superior supplement £25. Luxury room supplement £50. A variety of breaks are available at different times of year. Falconry centre, hovercraft, Dragon Boat racing, Honda Pilots.

Coniston Cold, Skipton, North Yorkshire BD23 4EA
T: (01756) 748080 **F:** (01756) 749487
E: reservations@theconistonhotel.com **W:** www.theconistonhotel.com

Nestled in the heart of the Yorkshire Dales, this property is part of the 1400-acre Coniston Estate. It is home to a shooting ground (CPSA Premier Plus), falconry centre, the Land Rover 4x4 experience, fly fishing on the 24-acre lake or river Aire. Archery, Walking and Cycling are also available. Maps are given to guests setting out on trails across the estate. Hotel facilities include free WIFI, making it an ideal place to meet for a business get-together or indeed to join up with friends and family. The Bannister suite caters for up to 150 banqueting guests or 200 conference delegates. The Huntsman's Lodge and Terrace is the perfect place to unwind, with stunning panoramic views of the Yorkshire Dales. Items such as morning coffee, lunch and afternoon tea are on the all-day menu. Alternatively guests can enjoy a meal in the popular Macleod's Restaurant. This serves a traditional array of home cooked foods from local produce or indeed from the estate itself.

DINING: 3 course table d'hôte dinner £32; à la carte, lunch & special diets available; last orders 2130; breakfast from 0730.

Site: ⚲ **P Payment:** 💳 **Leisure:** ♪ ▶ ☺ **Property:** ⊜ 🐟 🐕 ⊟ 🖥 🅿 ◐ ∅ **Children:** 🐾 🛏 🎠
Catering: 🍴🍷🍽 **Room:** 📶 ♨ 📞 📻 📺 ♿

RAITHWAITE ESTATE

Sandsend Road, Whitby, North Yorkshire YO21 3ST
T: (01947) 661661 F: (01947) 662662
E: reservations@raithwaiteestate.com W: www.raithwaiteestate.com

A grand country retreat comprising of two small luxury hotels and a collection of stunning private cottages located in Whitby, North Yorkshire. Spanning over 100 acres, the Raithwaite Estate is home to the Hall which is both traditional and luxurious, it comprises of 45 bedrooms including courtyard suites, The Keep, an exquisite 28 bedroom hotel; The Lake House, an ultra exclusive and luxurious 6 bedroom private property and The Fold, a collection of 7 beautifully designed stone built cottages. Whether you are looking for a relaxing break, a couples retreat, a romantic getaway or just time out from the city, this luxury hotel and cottage accommodation in the Whitby countryside has something for everyone. Features include the Spa, Brace Restaurant and Hunters Restaurant and two bars, Poachers Bar and Hunters Bar. For nature lovers the Estate has stunning gardens, a woodland with a number of walking routes and a relaxing Conservatory.

DINING: Avg meal price £35 for 3 courses in Brace Restaurant – à la carte –1800-2200. Poachers bar serves food as an alternative. 1200-2200 (booking not necessary). Sunday lunch is served in Brace restaurant 1200–1500. Private dining options available.

Site: ❀ P Payment: 💷 Leisure: 🎣 🏹 ⛵ 🎯 🎿 ♨ 🎾 Property: 🅿 🍽 🐾 🚆 🏧 🚵 ◗ Children: 🚸 🏩 🧗
Catering: (✕ 🍷 🍽 Room: 🍵 🐕 📞 📠 📺

BEDROOMS: 73
28 bedroom hotel, 45 bedrooms in the Hall, plus 6 bedroom private Lake House and 7 stone built cottages.

B&B PER ROOM PER NIGHT:
D: £125.00 - £515.00

ADDITIONAL INFORMATION:
The Estate's proximity to the coast and the North Yorkshire Moors provides guests with options to enjoy a variety of activities including archery, water sports, horse riding, shooting, mountain biking, guided walks and much more. The hotel is also dog friendly, and is home to North Yorkshire's first and only Dog Spa.

Cumbria

Lancashire

Greater Manchester

Merseyside

Cheshire

NORTH WEST
Cheshire, Cumbria, Lancashire, Greater Manchester, Merseyside

The breathtaking scenery of the Lake District dominates the North West, but urban attractions such as cosmopolitan Manchester and Liverpool, with its grand architecture and cultural credentials, have much to recommend them. Further afield, you can explore the Roman and Medieval heritage of Chester, discover Lancashire's wealth of historic houses and gardens, or make a date for one of the huge variety of events that take place in this region throughout the year.

115

NORTH WEST

Chester Castle

Old Dee Bridge

Museums

CHESHIRE

The charms of the old walled city of Chester and the picturesque villages that dot Cheshire's countryside contrast sharply with the industrial towns of Runcorn and Warrington.

Iron age forts, Roman ruins, Medieval churches, Tudor cottages and elegant Georgian and Victorian stately homes are among the many attractive sights of the county. South Cheshire, like Cumbria to the north, has long been the home of the wealthy from Manchester and Liverpool and boasts a huge selection of of excellent eateries. It also has peaceful, pretty countryside, and is within easy reach of the wilder terrain of the Peak District and North Wales.

Cholmondeley Castle Gardens
Malpas, Cheshire SY14 8AH
(01829) 720383
www.cholmondeleycastle.com
Among the most romantically beautiful gardens in the country. Visitors can enjoy the tranquil Temple Water Garden, Ruin Water Garden, memorial mosaic, Rose garden & many mixed borders.

CUMBRIA

In this lovely corner of England, there is beauty in breathtaking variety. The area is loved by many who come back time and again to its inspirational magic, brilliant blue lakes and craggy mountain tops. The central Lake District with its mountains, lakes and woods is so well known that there is a tendency to forget that the rest of Cumbria contains some of the most varied and attractive landscape in Britain. In the east of the county, the peaceful Eden Valley is sheltered by the towering hills of the Pennines, with charming little red sandstone villages and reminders of the Roman occupation everywhere. Alston, with its cobbled streets is the highest town in England, and has been used for numerous TV location sets.

Cumbria's long coastline is full of variety with rocky cliffs, sea birds, sandy estuaries, miles of sun-trap sand dunes and friendly harbours. In Autumn the deciduous woodlands and bracken coloured hillsides glow with colour. In Winter, the snow covered mountain tops dazzle magnificently against blue skies. In Spring, you can discover the delights of the

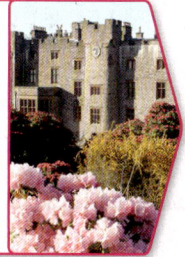

Muncaster Castle
Ravenglass, Cumbria CA18 1RQ
(01229) 717614
www.muncaster.co.uk
Medieval Muncaster Castle is a treasure trove of paintings, silver, embroideries and more. With acres of Grade 2 woodland gardens, famous for rhododendrons and breathtaking views of the Lake District.

magical, constantly changing light and the joy of finding carpets of wild flowers.

The Lake District is an outdoor enthusiasts paradise offering everything from walking and climbing to orienteering, potholing, cycling, riding, golf, sailing, sailboarding, canoeing, fishing and waterskiing. The Cumbrian climate is alsio ideal for gardens and the area is famous for the rhododendrons and azaleas which grow here in abundance. If you fancy a break from the great outdoors there is a wealth of historic houses, from small cottages where famous writers have lived, to stately homes that have seen centuries of gracious living and architectural importance.

LANCASHIRE

Lancashire's Forest of Bowland is an area of outstanding natural beauty with wild crags, superb walks, streams, valleys and fells. Blackpool on the coast has been the playground of the North West for many years and still draws millions of holiday makers every year. Morecambe, Southport, Lytham St Annes and Fleetwood also offer wide beaches, golf and bracing walks. Lancaster, a city since Roman times, has fine museums, a castle and an imitation of the Taj Mahal, the Ashton Memorial.

Browsholme Hall
Clitheroe, Lancashire BB7 3DE
(01254) 827160
www.browsholme.com
Built in 1507 and the ancestral Home of the Parker Family, Browsholme is a remarkable Tudor Hall with a major collection of oak furniture, portraits, glass, arms and armour. In 2010 an 18th Century 'tithe barn' was restored for refreshments, concerts, theatre, events and weddings.

MANCHESTER

Manchester's prosperity can be traced back to the 14th century when Flemish weavers arrived to transform a market town into a thriving boom city at the forefront of the Industrial Revolution. Now known as The Capital of the North, the city is rich in culture with plenty of galleries, museums, libraries and theatres.

Set in a stunning waterside location at the heart of the redeveloped Salford Quays in Greater Manchester, The Lowry is an architectural gem that brings together a wide variety of performing and visual arts, including the works of LS Lowry and contemporary exhibitions. The City Art Gallery displays its famous pre-Raphaelite collection while the Halle Orchestra regularly fills the Bridgewater Hall. Cosmopolitan Manchester makes a great place to stay for a spot of retail therapy too!

MERSEYSIDE

Liverpool was an important city long before The Beatles emerged from their Cavern in the Swinging Sixties. It grew from a village into a prosperous port, where emigrants sailed for the New World and immigrants arrived from Ireland. Today the ocean going liners are fewer, but the revitalised dock complex ensures that the city is as vibrant as ever. Liverpool's waterfront regeneration flagship is the Albert Dock Village, which includes the Maritime Museum and Tate Gallery Liverpool. The city has two modern cathedrals, a symphony orchestra, plenty of museums and Britain's oldest repertory theatre The Playhouse. In recent years, Liverpool has seen the opening of an extensive range of cafés, restaurants and accommodation to suit all tastes and budgets.

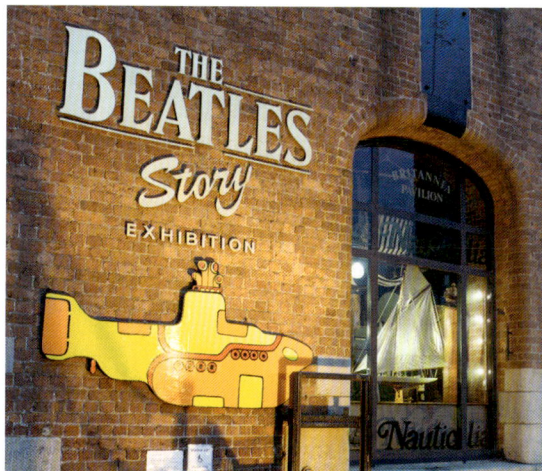

Walker Art Gallery
Liverpool, Merseyside L3 8EL
(0151) 478 4199
www.walkerartgallery.org.uk
Home to outstanding works by Rubens, Rembrandt, Poussin, Gainsborough and Hogarth, the Walker Art Gallery is one of the finest art galleries in Europe.

HUDSON'S HISTORIC HOUSES & GARDENS HIGHLIGHTS

Capesthorne Hall
(01625)861221
www.capesthorne.com
A spectacular venue, touched by nearly 1,000 years of history and set in 100 acres of picturesque Cheshire parkland.

Holker Hall & Gardens
(015395) 58328
www.holker.co.uk
Holker is the family home of Lord & Lady Cavendish. Steeped in history, this magnificent Victorian Mansion of neo-Elizabethan Gothic style was largely re-built in the 1870's following a fire, but origins date back to the 1600's.

Kirklinton Hall
(01697) 748850
www.kirklintonhall.co.uk
Adjacent to the 12th century de Boyville stronghold, Kirklinton Hall is said to have been built from its stone. The Hall has been a Restoration Great House, an RAF base, a school, a gangsters' gambling den and worse.

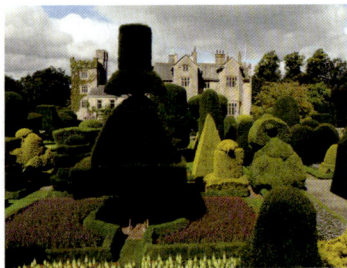

Leighton Hall
(01524) 734474
www.leightonhall.co.uk
Nestled in 1,550 acres of lush grounds, this romantic, Gothic house is the lived-in home of the famous Gillow furniture family.

Levens Hall & Gardens
(015395) 60321
www.levenshall.co.uk
An Elizabethan mansion built around a 13th century pele tower. The much loved home of the Bagot family.

Ness Botanic Gardens
0845 030 4063
www.nessgardens.org.uk
A beautiful 64 acre garden on the Dee estuary, founded by passionate plant hunter Arthur Kiplin Bulley.

Peover Hall & Gardens
(01565) 724220
www.peoverhall.com
A Grade 2 listed Elizabethan family house dating from 1585. Situated within some 500 acres of landscaped 18th century parkland with formal gardens.

Rode Hall & Gardens
(01270) 873237
www.rodehall.co.uk
The Wilbraham family have lived at Rode since 1669. The house stands in a Repton landscape and extensive gardens include a woodland garden which has many species of plants & flowers.

Tabley House
(01565) 750151
www.tableyhouse.co.uk
Tabley, a Grade I listed building, was designed by John Carr of York for the Leicester family. It contains one of the first collections of English paintings, including works of art by Turner, Reynolds, Lawrence, Lely and Dobson.

HUDSON'S
HISTORIC HOUSES & GARDENS
MUSEUMS & HERITAGE SITES

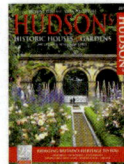

For more suggestions of great historic days out across Britain visit
www.hudsonsheritage.com

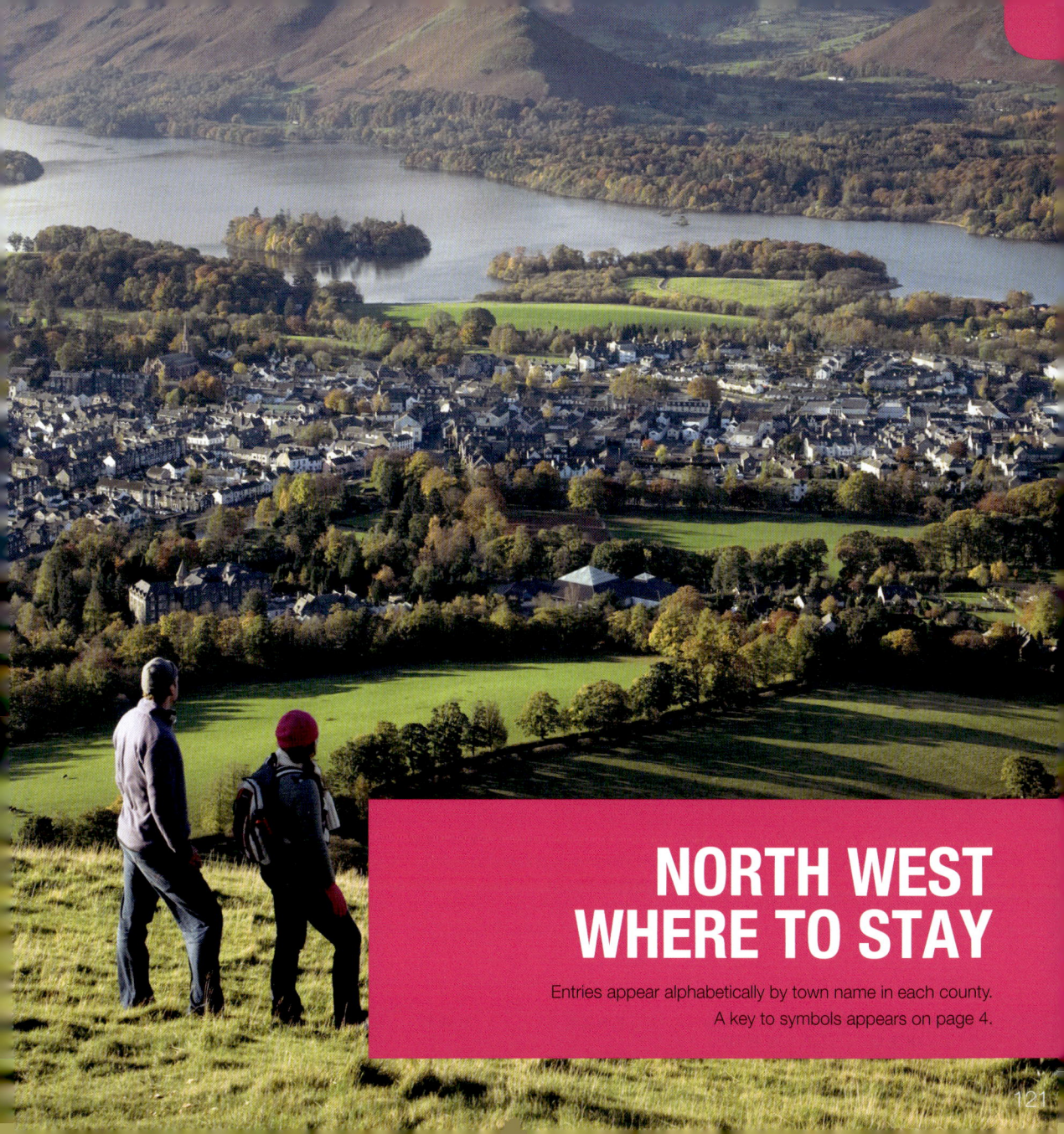

NORTH WEST
WHERE TO STAY

Entries appear alphabetically by town name in each county.
A key to symbols appears on page 4.

LOVELADY SHIELD COUNTRY HOUSE HOTEL

Nenthead Road, Alston, Cumbria CA9 3LF
T: (01434) 381203 **F:** (01434) 381515
E: enquiries@lovelady.co.uk **W:** www.lovelady.co.uk

Lovelady Shield. The name conjures up an image of the peace and tranquillity that you will certainly find in this gracious country house hotel. Set beside a river in a wooded valley high in the Pennines, just 2 1/4 miles from Alston (England's highest market town), this tranquil retreat is ideal for exploring the border country, the Lake District, Hadrian's Wall and the Yorkshire Dales. Only 35 minutes from the Penrith exit of the M6, via the dramatic A686 - one of the world's top drives - it is a very pleasant stopover. The owners, Mr & Mrs Haynes, together with their friendly staff, are maintaining the hotel's tradition of warm hospitality and service. Chef Anthony Muir's seasonal menus are imaginative and varied, using mostly local produce and the hotel has been awarded two AA Rosettes for the past five years for the high standard of the food. Service in the pretty dining room is discreet and attentive, and the hotel is well furnished and welcoming, with log fires. There are also two self-catering cottages in the grounds. A peaceful spot.

DINING: Table d'hôte dinner £47.50; bar lunches & special diets available; last orders 2030.

Site: ❀ P **Payment:** 💷 € **Leisure:** ♪ ▶ ♒ **Property:** 🎣 🐕 🖥 🅿 ⌀ **Children:** 🛝 🎮 ♀
Catering: ⓘ✕ 🍽 🍴 **Room:** 📞 📟 🎧 📺 📀

BEDROOMS: 12
The rooms in the extension have every comfort and amenity: DVD/CD players, power showers in the bathrooms and squishy duvets.

B&B PER ROOM PER NIGHT:
S: £85.00
D: £170.00

ADDITIONAL INFORMATION:
November–March, midweek, dinner, b&b from £140 per night for two people; weekend from £160 per person.

AYNSOME MANOR HOTEL

BEDROOMS: 10
The main house has 10 comfortable bedrooms mainly built around a courtyard, and covering two floors.

B&B PER ROOM PER NIGHT:
S: £80.00 - £135.00
D: £90.00 - £147.00

ADDITIONAL INFORMATION:
Please see website for any special offers. Open February - December. Located in the still untouched Vale of Cartmel and with views southwards to the Norman Priory, meadowlands and woods, Aynsome Manor represents an ideal centre from which to explore the area.

Cartmel, Grange-over-Sands, Cumbria LA11 6HH
T: (015395) 36653 **F:** (015395) 36016
E: aynsomemanor@btconnect.com **W:** www.aynsomemanorhotel.co.uk

The age of elegance is not past; it still lives on at this lovely old manor house where two generations of the Varley family have created a special atmosphere of warmth and comfort. Once the distinguished residence of the descendants of William Marshall, the Earl of Pembroke, founder of the historic 12th Century Cartmel Priory, Aynsome still echoes with the character and traditions of that bygone era. The candle lit dining room creates an ideal setting for a relaxed meal where guests can enjoy the imaginative and carefully chosen table hotel menu, changed daily using fresh local produce. Service will be attentive, without being obtrusive. Good food is extremely important at Aynsome and constant attention ensures commendable ratings in the independent guide books. Local produce, imaginative menus and professional expertise will enable you to approach each meal with anticipation. Chris, Andrea and their dedicated team will ensure a warm welcome to both Aynsome Manor Hotel and Cartmel. "A vibrant village in every season with an ancient medieval heart".

DINING: Table d'hôte 3 course dinner £29.50. Special diets catered for. Last orders 2030. Breakfast 0815 - 0945.

Site: P **Payment:** 💳 **Property:** 🐾 📺 🖉 **Children:** 🐎 🎏 **Catering:** 🍴 🍷 **Room:** 🫖 💧 ☎ 📺

OAK BANK HOTEL

Broadgate, Grasmere Village, Lake District, Cumbria LA22 9TA
T: (015394) 35217 **F:** (015394) 35685
E: info@lakedistricthotel.co.uk **W:** www.lakedistricthotel.co.uk

Like many hotels in the Lake District, Oak Bank was originally a private merchant's house built in 1872. It became a hotel in 1920 and its central location in the heart of Grasmere puts all the Lake District attractions within easy reach. It is a short walk from St Oswald's Church, final resting place of William Wordsworth whose Daffodil Garden and Dove Cottage are nearby. Glynis and Simon Wood own and personally manage Oak Bank, ably assisted by a small band of loyal staff including Head chef Darren Cornish, who presides over the AA two Rosette Restaurant. This has become a destination in its own right, using top quality fresh ingredients, locally sourced where possible. They make their own bread, pasta, sauces, jus and sorbets. A selection of fine wines from around the world is available to complement the dining experience. The dining room overlooks the hotel garden, a short walk down to the river Rothay which flows on into Grasmere lake.

DINING: 3 course table d'hôte dinner £38; à la carte available; lunch available; vegetarian & special diets available; last orders 2000; breakfast from 0815.

BEDROOMS: 13
Rooms to suit all tastes and budgets, from standard double to superior four poster and the superb Acorn Suite. All bedrooms are individually and stylishly decorated, with flat screen TV, luxury toiletries and hospitality tray.

B&B PER ROOM PER NIGHT:
S: £70.75
D: £65.50

ADDITIONAL INFORMATION:
Open all year. Wi-Fi available. Single rate is based on single occupancy of a double room.

Site: ✿ Payment: 💳 Leisure: 🎵 ▸ ♻ ✗ Property: ⊛ 🐾 ⊟ 🗄 ♨ ⊘ Children: 🍴 🛏 ☂
Catering: 🍴✗ 🍷 🍽 Room: 🗑 ⬦ ☎ 📺

AA
★★★
Hotel

BORROWDALE GATES HOTEL

BEDROOMS: 25
10 bedrooms on ground floor.

B&B PER ROOM PER NIGHT:
S: £61.00 - £93.00
D: £122.00 - £206.00

ADDITIONAL INFORMATION:
Single room with breakfast from £61;
double from £122. Specialised
weekend and other breaks available –
see website for details.

Grange-in-Borrowdale, Keswick, Cumbria CA12 5UQ
T: (01768) 777204 **F:** (01768) 777195
E: hotel@borrowdale-gates.com **W:** www.borrowdale-gates.com

Originally a private residence situated on the edge of the historic hamlet of Grange,
Borrowdale Gates maintains the lovely homely atmosphere of a genuine country house,
where the cares of the world just ebb away. Location is sublime. Set in two acres of wooded
gardens, with a backdrop of high, rising fells, close to the shores of Derwentwater, the hotel
offers seclusion without remoteness. Its aspect is perfect, providing panoramic views of the
dramatic lakeland scenery. Wonderful lakeland cooking, an outstanding wine list and personal
service all combine to create a memorable guest experience. The lounges have picture
length windows and log fires and make an ideal place to read, chat or enjoy afternoon tea.
Bedrooms, ten of which are on the ground floor, have every amenity and are wonderful to
return to after a day's invigorating walking or sightseeing. All have views of the surrounding
valley, fells or farmland. Guests can also relax in the gardens with unspoiled views of Castle
Crag, the famous Jaws of Borrowdale and the distant Scafell Pike.

DINING: 3 course table d'hôte dinner £39. À la carte, lunch & special diets available; Last
orders 2030; breakfast from 0800.

Site: ❀ P **Payment:** 💳 **Leisure:** 🎣 ▶ ↻ **Property:** 🐕 🖼 **Room:** ♿

GILPIN HOTEL & LAKE HOUSE

Crook Road, Windermere, Cumbria LA23 3NE
T: (015394) 88818 F: (015394) 88058
E: hotel@thegilpin.co.uk W: www.thegilpin.co.uk

Meticulously run by the Cunliffe family, Gilpin Hotel is set in 20 tranquil acres of woodland, moor and country gardens. The family is assisted by a team of dedicated, long serving staff whose experience shows at every corner. Just 12 miles from the M6, almost opposite Windermere Golf Course ('the miniature Gleneagles'), this four-star Relais & Chateaux hotel is at the heart of the Lake District's wealth of sightseeing, heritage and activities. The Gilpin Lake House (a mile away) sits on its own four-acre lake with private spa, boat-house, boat, cedarwood hot tub, indoor pool, salt snug and 100 acres of private gardens and grounds. Accommodation consists of six suites which exclusively share these facilities (the house can also be booked for exclusive use). A chauffeur will take guests to the main hotel, where they can enjoy three AA Rosette cuisine, skilfully prepared using top quality ingredients with an excellent balance of fresh vibrant flavours and textures, with a contemporary slant.

DINING: 4 course table d'hôte dinner £58; 3 course Sunday lunch £35; à la carte 3 course lunch from £30.

BEDROOMS: 26
Seven rooms lead directly onto the gardens and a further six Garden Suites have hot tubs, all of the rooms are spacious, quiet, with lovely views and constant refurbishment. As in the main house, decor by Christine Cunliffe uses exquisite fabrics, wonderful upholstery, with delicious art on the walls and luxurious bathrooms.

B&B PER ROOM PER NIGHT:
S: £235.00 - £525.00
D: £255.00 - £535.00

ADDITIONAL INFORMATION:
Open all year.

Site: ✿ P Payment: 💷 Leisure: 🎣 ⚑ ✗ Property: 📺 📗 ◑ ⌀ Children: ⌖ Catering: ⟨✗ ♟ 🍴 Room: 🖥 🚰 📞

HOLBECK GHYLL COUNTRY HOUSE HOTEL

BEDROOMS: 27
Bedrooms contain decanters of locally-distilled damson gin, fresh flowers, luxurious Egyptian cotton sheets and robes, private terraces and hot tubs.

B&B PER ROOM PER NIGHT:
S: £150.00 - £245.00
D: £170.00 - £390.00

ADDITIONAL INFORMATION:
The boutique Spa, with sauna, steam room and heated outdoor hot tub features stunning views across to the Langdales Pikes and Coniston Old Man, perfect for relaxing into at the end of the day.

Holbeck Lane, Windermere, Cumbria LA23 1LU
T: (01539) 432375 **F:** (01539) 434743
E: stay@holbeckghyll.com **W:** www.holbeckghyll.com

Holbeck is more like a beautiful private home than a hotel, with no two of our richly-appointed rooms the same. Whether you choose to sink into an armchair by the inglenook fireplace with the morning's newspaper, or rest your fell-weary limbs in one of the sumptuous lounges overlooking the Lake District in all its glory, you'll find the perfect spot to recharge your batteries. There are 13 beautiful rooms and suites in the main house, 6 exquisite rooms in The Lodge, 3 luxury cottages, 4 fabulous suites and our splendid Miss Potter suite where Hollywood star Renée Zellweger lived during filming of the movie about Beatrix Potter's life. Bedrooms enjoy an intoxicating view over Windermere that has been voted among the top 15 in the world.

DINING: The head chef David McLaughlin, has built a reputation around serving the very finest ingredients.

Payment: ▭ **Leisure:** ▶ ✕ ⚲ ☄ ⚲ **Property:** ♟ ✕ ⊟ ▣ ⚲ ◌ **Children:** ⚲ ▥ ✕ **Catering:** ◖✕ ⚲
Room: ⚲ ☎ ◎ 📺

NORTH EAST
County Durham, Northumberland, Tees Valley, Tyne & Wear

Northumberland

Tyne & Wear

County Durham

Tees Valley

The North East contains two Areas of Outstanding Natural Beauty, a National Park, Hadrian's Wall, the dynamic city of Newcastle, and County Durham, with its fine cathedral and castle. This region is awash with dramatic hills, sweeping valleys, vast expanses of dune-fringed beaches and ragged cliffs with spectacular views. Littered with dramatic castles, ruins and historic houses, there are plenty of exciting family attractions and walking routes galore.

NORTH EAST

COUNTY DURHAM & TEES VALLEY

Durham Cathedral, the greatest Norman building in England, was once a prison and soars grandly above the Medieval city and surrounding plain. Famed for its location as much as for its architecture, it is the burial place of both St Cuthbert, a great northern saint, and the Venerable Bede, author of the first English history.

The Vale of Durham is packed full of award-winning attractions including Locomotion: The National Railway Museum at Shildon and Beamish – The Living Museum of the North, the country's largest open air museum. Auckland Castle was the palace of Durham's unique Prince Bishops for more than 900 years. Part of the North Pennines Area of Outstanding Natural Beauty, the Durham Dales including Teesdale and Weardale, is a beautiful landscape of hills, moors, valleys and rivers, with numerous picturesque villages and market towns.

Raby Castle
Staindrop, County Durham DL2 3AH
(01833) 660202
www.rabycastle.com
Home of Lord Barnard's family since 1626, includes a 200 acre deer park, gardens, carriage collection, adventure playground, shop and tearoom.

The Durham Heritage Coast, from Sunderland to Hartlepool, is one of the finest in England. The coastal path that runs along much of its length takes you on a spectacular journey of natural, historical and geological interest, with dramatic views along the shore and out over the North Sea. The historic port city of Hartlepool has award-winning attractions, a fantastic marina, beaches and countryside.

Comprising miles of stunning coastline and acres of ancient woodland, Tees Valley covers the lower, flatter area of the valley of the River Tees. This unique part of the UK, split between County Durham and Yorkshire, has nearly a hundred visitor attractions, including Preston Hall and Saltholme Nature Reserve, which can both be found in Stockton-on-Tees.

Beamish Museum
County Durham DH9 0RG
(01913) 704000
www.beamish.org.uk

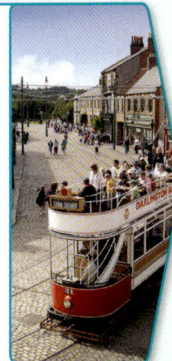

Beamish - The Living Museum of the North, is a world-famous open air museum vividly recreating life in the North East in the early 1800's and 1900's. It tells the story of the people of North East England during the Georgian, Victorian, and Edwardian periods through a costumed cast, engaging exhibits and an exciting programme of events.

NEWCASTLE & TYNE AND WEAR

Newcastle-upon-Tyne, once a shipbuilding centre, is a rejuvenated city of proud civic tradition with fine restaurants, theatres, and one of the liveliest arts scenes outside London.

Housed in a landmark industrial building on the south bank of the River Tyne in Gateshead, BALTIC is a major international centre for contemporary art and is the biggest gallery of its kind in the world. It presents a dynamic, diverse and international programme of contemporary visual art, ranging from blockbuster exhibitions to innovative new work and projects created by artists working within the local community.

Sage Gateshead
Gateshead, Tyne and Wear NE8 2JR
(0191) 443 4661
www.sagegateshead.com
The Sage Gateshead is a concert venue and centre for musical education on the south bank of the River Tyne. It stages a varied and eclectic programme in state-of-the-art halls.

As well as the BALTIC, there's the Laing Art Gallery and the Great North Museum. The Theatre Royal is the third home of the Royal Shakespeare Company and a venue for major touring companies. The Metro Centre in neighbouring Gateshead attracts shoppers from all over the country with more than 300 outlets and 11 cinema screens.

NORTHUMBERLAND

Northumbria, to use its ancient name, is an undiscovered holiday paradise where the scenery is wild and beautiful, the beaches golden and unspoiled, and the natives friendly. The region is edged by the North Sea, four national parks and the vast Border Forest Park. Its eastern sea boundary makes a stunning coastline, stretching 100 miles from Staithes on the Cleveland boundary, to Berwick-on-Tweed, England's most northerly town, frequently fought over and with the finest preserved example of Elizabethan town walls in the country. In between you'll find as many holiday opportunities as changes of scenery.

Step back in time 2,000 years along Hadrian's Wall, explore the hills, forests and waterfalls of the National Parks, and discover historic castles, splendid churches and quaint towns. Visitors can trace man's occupation of the region from prehistoric times through rock carvings, ancient hill forts, Saxon churches, Norman priories, medieval castles, and a wealth of industrial archaeology. Housesteads Roman Fort at Haydon Bridge is the most complete example of a British Roman fort. It features magnificent ruins and stunning views of the countryside surrounding Hadrian's Wall.

Alnwick Castle and Alnwick Castle Gardens are both well worth a visit if you are up this way, as is Chillingham Castle with its splendid views and romantic gardens. The region has a rich maritime heritage too. Ruined coastal fortifications such as Dunstanburgh and fairy-tale Lindisfarne are relics of a turbulent era. Agriculture is also one of the region's most important industries. Take a trip on the Heatherslaw Light Railway, a narrow gauge line operating from Etal Village to Heatherslaw Mill, a restored waterdriven corn mill and agricultural museum near the delightful model village of Ford.

Lindisfarne Priory
Holy Island,
Northumberland TD15 2RX
(01289) 389200
www.english-heritage.org.uk
Lying just a few miles off the beautiful Northumberland coast, Holy Island contains a wealth of history and is home to one of the region's most revered treasures, Lindisfarne Priory. The epicentre of Christianity in Anglo Saxon times and once the home of St Oswald, it was the birthplace of the Lindisfarne Gospels, one of the world's most precious books and remains a place of pilgrimage today.

HUDSON'S HISTORIC HOUSES & GARDENS HIGHLIGHTS

Alnwick Castle
(01665) 511100
www.alnwickcastle.com
Home to the Duke of Northumberland's family, the Percys, for over 700 years; offers history on a grand scale.

The Alnwick Garden
(01665) 511350
www.alnwickgarden.com
The Alnwick Garden combines provocative and traditional landscapes in the heart of Northumberland.

Auckland Castle
(01388) 743750
www.aucklandcastle.org
Auckland Castle is one of the best preserved Medieval Bishop's Palaces in Europe.

Bamburgh Castle
(01668) 214208
www.bamburghcastle.com
These formidable stone walls have witnessed dark tales of royal rebellion, bloody battles, spellbinding legends and millionaire benefactors. With fourteen public rooms and 3000 artefacts, including arms and armour, porcelain, furniture and artwork.

The Bowes Museum
(01833) 690606
www.thebowesmuseum.org.uk
Set in beautiful grounds, the transformed museum houses fine art, fashion and textiles, ceramics and furniture.

Chillingham Castle
(01668) 215359
www.chillingham-castle.com
20 Minutes from seaside or mountains. 4 stars in Simon Jenkins' 'Thousand Best Houses' and the very first of The Independent's '50 Best Castles in Britain & Ireland'.

Durham Cathedral
(0191) 3864266
www.durhamcathedral.co.uk
A world heritage site and burial place of St Cuthbert and the Venerable Bede.

Newcastle Castle
(0191) 2306300
www.newcastlecastle.co.uk
This fine medieval castle is steeped in nearly 1000 years of history.

Preston Tower
07966 150216
www.prestontower.co.uk
Built between 1392 and 1399 it was one of the 78 Pele Towers in Northumberland. Some rooms furnished as they may have been in the 14th Century.

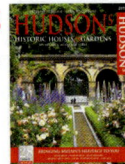

HUDSON'S
HISTORIC HOUSES & GARDENS
MUSEUMS & HERITAGE SITES

For more suggestions of great historic days out across Britain visit
www.hudsonsheritage.com

NORTH EAST
WHERE TO STAY

Entries appear alphabetically by town name in each county.

A key to symbols appears on page 4.

WAREN HOUSE HOTEL

Waren Mill, Bamburgh, Northumberland NE70 7EE
T: (01668) 214581 **F:** (01668) 214484
E: enquiries@warenhousehotel.co.uk **W:** www.warenhousehotel.co.uk

Set in six acres of gardens and woodland, Waren House is a peaceful and tranquil centre from which to visit one of this country's most naturally beautiful and historic areas, largely unspoiled by tourism and commercialism. The castles of Bamburgh, Dunstanburgh, Alnwick and Warkworth are all easily accessible. The Holy Island of Lindisfarne is nearby. There is a wealth of birdlife along miles of magnificent coastline, particularly at Budle Bay and the Farne Islands. After a day's sightseeing, you can return to the quiet luxury of Waren House where owners Peter and Anita Laverack and their staff will pamper you and enjoy the garden with the Roman statues. In the evening guests can enjoy a gastronomic treat in Grays Restaurant, a favourite with locals and residents alike under the supervision of Steve Ownes. Specialising in locally sourced ingredients, it has been awarded one AA Rosette. As you enjoy the hospitality, reflect on your good fortune at having stopped here, rather than speeding by without discovering the splendours of this historic region and of Waren House in particular.

DINING: Table d'hôte dinner £42; special diets available; last orders 2030.

BEDROOMS: 15
The hotel offers three suites and 12 individually styled bedrooms, including some ground floor.

B&B PER ROOM PER NIGHT:
S: £90.00 - £155.00
D: £130.00 - £250.00

ADDITIONAL INFORMATION:
Two nights, 5 course dinner, b&b from £170 per room per night.

Site: P Payment: 💳 **Leisure:** ⚲ ↺ **Property:** 🐾 🖼 **Room:** ♨ 📻

SCOTLAND

Scotland is a proud nation with much to be proud of, from famous inventors, writers, politicians and a resplendent history, to dramatic mountains, stunningly beautiful countryside, a breathtaking coastline and islands of every character. Golf was invented at St Andrews four centuries ago and the whole of Scotland is a playground for walkers, golfers, sailors, fishermen, skiers and other outdoor enthusiasts. If heritage is your thing, there's nowhere quite like this land of majestic castles, historic houses, grand gardens and atmospheric ruins. Alive with wildlife, heritage, culture, food and much more - a trip to Scotland is unforgettable.

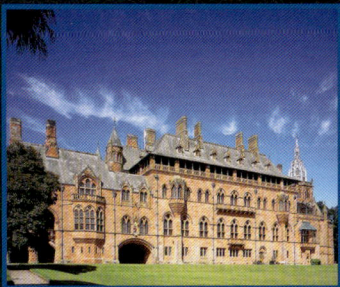

SCOTLAND

ABERDEEN CITY & SHIRE

A place where majestic landscapes meet the sea and the flourishing Granite City boasts beautiful architecture and cultural gems, and of course much beloved by the Royal Family who have their holiday home at Balmoral Castle. There are too many castles to list and many fine houses too, including Cairness House near Fraserburgh and the magnificent Georgian Duff House in Banff. With rolling countryside, lush forests and woodlands, sandy beaches and magnificent mountains to explore, this is one of Scotland's most captivating regions. The excellent Coastal Trail covers the breathtaking north east coastline while The Victorian Heritage Trail is the perfect way to explore Royal Deeside. The breathtakingly beautiful Cairngorms National Park are within easy reach of the city and there are plenty of charming towns and villages, together with a wealth of outdoor activities and remarkable wildlife.

Balmoral Castle
Aberdeenshire AB35 5TB
(01339) 742534
www.balmoralcastle.com
The spectacular Scottish holiday home of the Royal Family.

ARGYLL & THE ISLES

Enjoy stunning coastal and Highland scenery, wildlife, watersports, historic monuments, fascinating museums and lush gardens. Visit the imposing Inveraray Castle, a Clan Campbell stronghold since the time of King Robert the Bruce and the enchanting Benmore Botanic Garden, in its magnificent mountainside setting on the Cowal Peninsula. Bustling Oban overlooks Oban Bay and is well known as the

Gateway to the Outer and Inner Hebrides. The range of inter-island ferries is a great way to explore. On Mull, across the water from Oban, the picture-postcard town of Tobermory is famous for its colourful waterfront houses.

AYRSHIRE & ARRAN

The vivid greens of Ayrshire's rich pastures contrast strikingly with the steep mountainous profile of Arran as a backdrop. Discover ancient history and heritage, tantalise your tastebuds with fine food and whiskies, or enjoy the many outdoor pursuits and exciting events on offer. The 18th century Dumfries House and splendid Dean Castle and Country Park in Kilmarnock are must-visit attractions. Arran's heritage dates back to the Stone Age and evidence of this can still be seen at sites such as the stone circles at Machrie Moor. Brodick Castle, set dramatically against the backdrop of Goat Fell Mountain, has stunning views over Brodick Bay to the Firth of Clyde.

DUMFRIES & GALLOWAY

From sparkling streams and spectacular summits to lush forests and sandy shores, the landscape here is naturally inspiring. The region's history, culture and beautiful scenery has filled artists and writers with the passion to create great works and it is the perfect setting for exciting activities and rare wildlife. With so much inspiration around, it's not surprising that the region boasts a thriving arts and culture scene. Once the home of Robert Burns, today Dumfries & Galloway continues to inspire modern artists and craftsmen.

DUNDEE & ANGUS

Enjoy the best of both worlds in Dundee & Angus where cosmoplitan city attractions rub shouders with majestic glens, pristine beaches and ancient forests perfect for walking and fishing. Uncover a captivating history, fantastic golf courses and a wide range of events and festivals. Visitor attractions include RRS Discovery, the ship which took Captain Scott on his remarkable voyage to Antarctica, and HMS Frigate Unicorn, a preserved warship which was first launched in 1824 and is the sixth oldest ship in the world.

EDINBURGH & THE LOTHIANS

Edinburgh is the jewel in Scotland's crown with fortified hilltop architecture, sweeping Georgian crescents, medieval cobbled streets, graceful bridges spanning chasms and green parks. Its centrepiece is the ancient Castle and some of the best scenery can be found in Holyrood Park, dominated by Arthur's Seat, the most impressive of the volcanoes. The 18th century New Town is recognised as the largest single area of Georgian architecture in Europe, while the National Gallery of Scotland and the Scottish National Gallery of Modern Art house two of Britain's finest collections of paintings. Today the highlight of Edinburgh's cultural year is the Edinburgh Festival, the largest pan-arts festival in the world, and its 500+ 'fringe' events.

Edinburgh Castle
Edinburgh EH1 2NG
(0131) 225 9846
www.edinburghcastle.gov.uk
Dominating the skyline from its perch on an extinct volcano, Edinburgh castle houses plenty of attractions including The Honours of Scotland and The Stone of Destiny - coronation stone of Scotland's ancient kings.

Leith is the city's medieval port, now home to the former royal yacht Britannia. The surrounding Lothians are made up of gently rolling countryside, pretty towns and villages and an impressive collection of historic castle remains.

GLASGOW & THE CLYDE VALLEY

Glasgow, Scotland's 'Second Capital' and largest city, has been reborn as a vibrant centre of style against a backdrop of exceptional Victorian architecture. First-class events, world famous art collections, free attractions and beautiful parks and gardens abound. The Cathedral, The Riverside Museum and revitalised riverside area all attract visitors. Kelvingrove Park contains Kelvingrove Art Gallery and Museum, a unique collection of European art, arms and armour. The Botanic Gardens has the amazing Kibble Palace, an ornate Victorian glasshouse full of tropical plants from around the world, while Glasgow Green is home to the People's Palace social history museum. Further afield, the 42-mile long Clyde Valley driving route follows the River Clyde through spectacular countryside towards Lanark. Attractions include the World Heritage Site of New Lanark model industrial community, and the scenic Falls of Clyde. Dams to Darnley has over 1,350 acres of water, wetland, woodland and grassland including the striking Barrhead dams. Scotland's largest regional park, Clyde Muirshiel, sits to the west and the RSPB Nature Reserve at Lochwinnoch is a great place to enjoy the region's wildlife.

THE HIGHLANDS & SKYE

The Highlands are famed for magnificent mountains, glens and lochs - think Ben Nevis and Loch Ness. Add in sandy beaches, stunning islands and and fascinating history for a truly inspiring region. Follow one of VisitScotland's established trails such as the Moray Coast trail, or spend a few days visiting the region's historic castles, monuments and battlefields. The Glenfinnan Monument, at the head of Loch Shiel, is a tribute to the history of the Jacobite Rebellion led by Bonnie Prince Charlie. Walk the battlefield at Culloden and get vivid details of the Jacobites' 1746 defeat by government troops at the visitor centre. Fort George, built by the government in the wake of Culloden, is one of the finest feats of 18th century military engineering. Inverness is great for a relaxing city break - take a peaceful stroll along the banks of the River Ness, visit Inverness Castle, St Andrew's Cathedral, and the Botanic Gardens for stunning flowers and the indoor waterfall.

Isle of Skye
Scottish Highlands
www.visitscotland.com
The largest and best known of the Inner Hebrides is renowned for its natural Highland beauty, with sparkling lochs, heather-clad moors and the towering Cuillin Mountains.

THE KINGDOM OF FIFE

Compact Fife boasts a wonderful mix of stunning scenery and miles of dedicated cycling and walking routes. Try the Kingdom of Fife Millenium Cycle Ways or the spectacular 117 miles (188 km) long Fife Coastal Path. Falkland Palace is a former royal palace of the Scottish Kings and Culross Palace is adorned with fine painted ceilings and antique furniture. Head to the Lomond Hills Regional Park to see geological marvels such as the bizarrely shaped Bonnet Stane and Carlin Maggie's Stane. Play a round of golf or head to the beach - Fife is home to all three of Scotland's Blue Flag beaches: Elie Ruby Bay, Aberdour Silver Sands and Burntisland.

LOCH LOMOND, THE TROSSACHS, STIRLING & THE FORTH VALLEY

Visit this diverse region for famous castles, an exciting safari park, outdoor adventures and more. Doune Castle near Stirling is a magnificent 14th century courtyard castle with an intriguing movie connection. Callendar House in Falkirk is one of Scotland's finest baronial mansions where Mary Queen of Scots spent much of her early life.

ORKNEY

Around seventy islands and skerries make up Orkney, with its incredible scenery, coastline, wildlife and archaeological sites. This was an important seat of power in the Viking Empire, reflected by the magnificent 12th century cathedral of St Magnus in Kirkwall and distinctly Scandinavian place names. The Ring of Brodgar and the Standing Stones of Stenness, in the Heart of Neolithic Orkney World Heritage Site, are some of the best-preserved sites in Europe. These days, with craft jewellers and artists drawing inspiration from the landscape and history, Orkney has a thriving arts and crafts scene and the islands are also heaven for food lovers.

OUTER HEBRIDES

The Outer Hebrides is a paradise of powder white beaches, Atlantic waves, dark moorland, rugged mountains and amazing wildlife. This idyllic chain of 200 inter-linked islands sits 30 miles off the north west coast of Scotland and is the perfect destination for walking, cycling, golfing, fishing, sightseeing and soaking up a rich and vibrant history. From the magnificent Calanais Standing Stones on Lewis and Bosta Iron Age House on Great Bernera to the contrasting terrain of low lying Lewis and mountainous Harris, the islands offer unique archaeology and great outdoor adventures. Visit St Kilda for amazing birdwatching or sample Hebridean delicacies such as Stornoway black pudding.

PERTHSHIRE

Explore majestic glens, championship golf courses and ancient forests. Discover centuries of history, adrenaline-packed adventure, and delicious food and drink. Visit the original home of the legendary Stone of Destiny at Scone Palace or the ruined tower house where Mary Queen of Scots was incarcerated on Castle Island at Loch Leven in 1567. Uncover the 300-year-old history of the Black Watch regiment at Balhousie Castle, or step inside a fantastically recreated Iron-Age dwelling at the Scottish Crannog Centre on Loch Tay. Culture vultures should visit Perth Museum and Art Gallery and The Pitlochry Festival Theatre, one of Scotland's finest theatrical institutions on the banks of the River Tay.

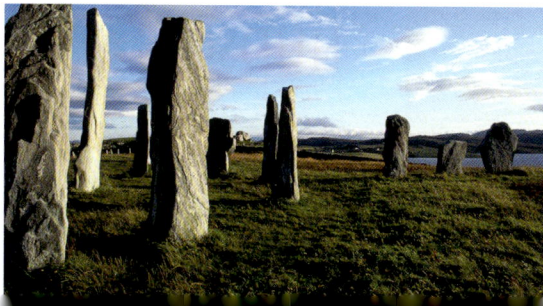

Blair Castle, Pitlochry, Perthshire
PH18 5TL (01796) 481207
www.blair-castle.co.uk
Explore the region's Jacobite past at Blair Castle where Bonnie Prince Charlie stayed during the Jacobite rising of 1745.

SCOTTISH BORDERS

It's easy to lose yourself amongst the spectacular scenery of the Scottish Borders. The Tweed meanders from the coast along the border to rise in the Pentland Hills and the hazy blue peaks of the Elidon Hills have lifted the hearts of many a northbound traveller. En route from Carlisle towards Edinburgh, you will pass Bruce's Cave and numerous castle remains where he fought the English. The A7 scenic route passes through the gentle hills of Eskdale and the Moorfoots and you can take in Borders' dramatic history and culture at ruined castles and exciting festivals. Delight in the thriving arts and crafts scene, enjoy delicious local produce and explore miles of rolling hills, leafy valleys and beautiful coast.

SHETLAND

Classified as a global Geopark, this cluster of over 100 wild, awe-inspiring islands provide endless inspiration for artists and photographers. Inhabited for over 6,000 years, archaeology, dialect (based on old Scots and Norse), place names, food and world-renowned traditional music all help to tell the story of Shetland's unique history. The Jarlshof is a record of human occupation going back 5,000 years, and the influence of Scandinavia is everywhere. The wildlife here is truly wild with otters, seals, bird and whale-watching, and there is a wealth of things to see and do all across Shetland, so be sure to visit more than just the mainland. Unst, Yell, Fetlar and the more outlying islands are equally impressive and offer very different experiences.

HUDSON'S HISTORIC HOUSES & GARDENS HIGHLIGHTS

Cawdor Castle
(01667) 404401
www.cawdorcastle.com
A must see romantic fairy-tale Castle of historical beauty and one of the most outstanding Stately Homes in Scotland.

Dalmeny House
(0131 331) 1888
www.dalmeny.co.uk
A family home which contains Scotland's finest French treasurers. Dine in splendor, and enjoy sea-views over superb parkland.

Dumfries House
(01290) 425959
www.dumfries-house.org.uk
A Georgian Gem, nesting within 2,000 acres of scenic Ayrshire countryside in south west Scotland.

Dunvegan Castle & Gardens
(01470) 521206
www.dunvegancastle.com
Experience living history at Dunvegan Castle, the ancestral home of the Chiefs of Clan MacLeod for 800 years.

Floors Castle
(01573) 223333
www.floorscastle.com
Spectacular state rooms with an outstanding collection of paintings, furniture and tapestries. Picturesque grounds and walled gardens.

Hopetoun House
(0131) 331 2451
www.hopetoun.co.uk
A unique gem of Europe's architectural heritage and undoubtedly 'Scotland's Finest Stately Home'.

Inveraray Castle & Garden
(01499) 302203
www.inveraray-castle.com
Home to the Duke & Duchess of Argyll and ancestral home of the Clan Campbell.

Manderston
(01361) 883450
www.manderston.co.uk
With its magnificent stables, stunning marble dairy and 56 acres of immaculate gardens.

Mount Stuart
(01700) 503877
www.mountstuart.com
Ancestral home of the Marquess of Bute, is a stupendous example of Victorian Gothic architecture set amidst 300 acres of gloriously landscaped gardens.

Stirling Castle
(01786) 450000
www.stirlingcastle.gov.uk
Explore the richly decorated King's and Queen's apartments. Take the guided tour where you can hear tales of the castle's history.

HUDSON'S
HISTORIC HOUSES & GARDENS
MUSEUMS & HERITAGE SITES

For more suggestions of great historic days out across Britain visit
www.hudsonsheritage.com

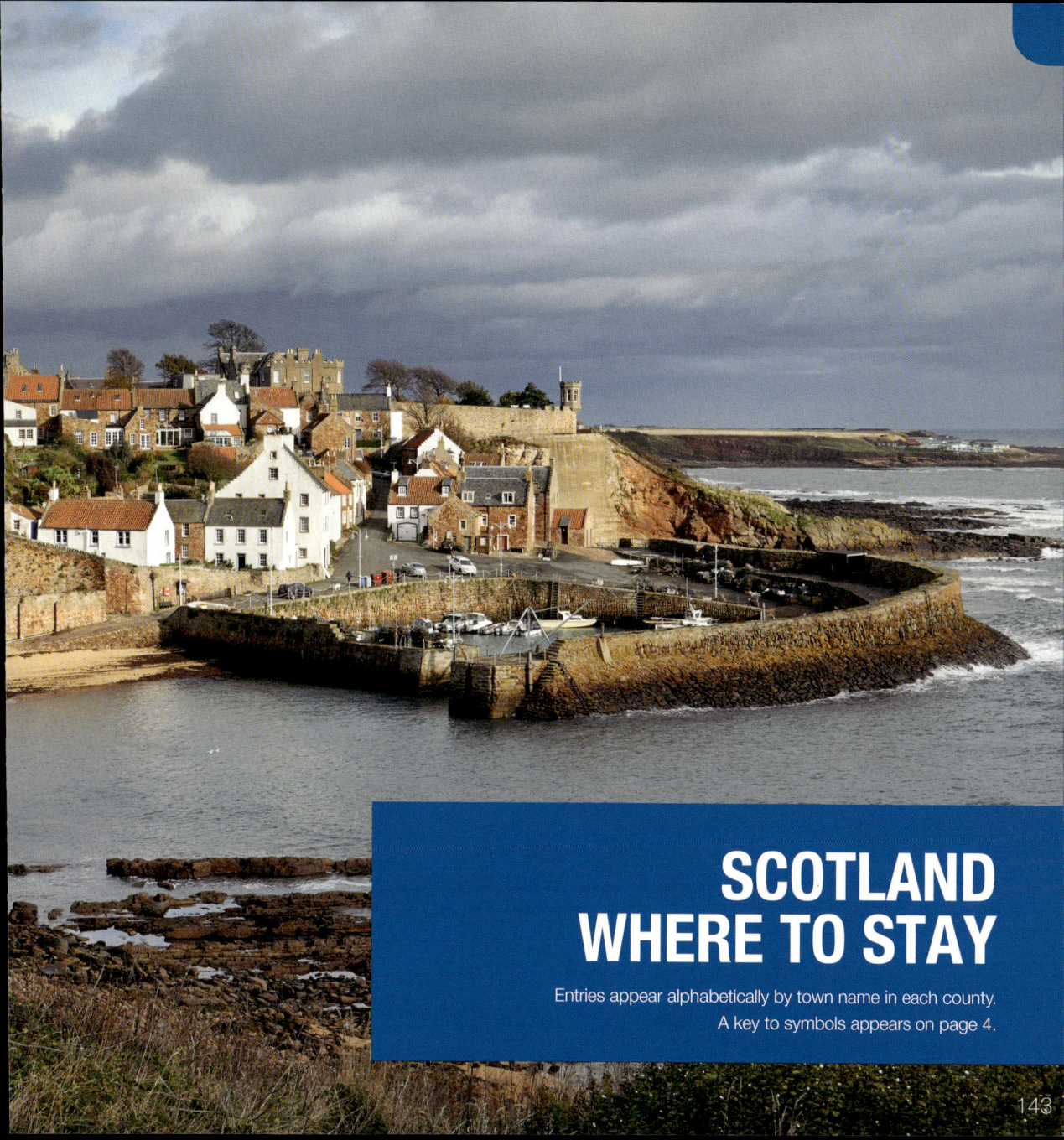

SCOTLAND
WHERE TO STAY

Entries appear alphabetically by town name in each county.

A key to symbols appears on page 4.

LOCH MELFORT HOTEL

Arduaine, Oban, Argyll and Bute, Scotland PA34 4XG
T: (01852) 200233 **F:** (01852) 200214
E: reception@lochmelfort.co.uk **W:** www.lochmelfort.co.uk

Loch Melfort Hotel is a unique retreat set in 17 acres of the romantic Gulf Stream-warmed coast of Argyll. It has recently been bought by Calum and Rachel Ross who have already made quite an impression! Public rooms have been upgraded and are ideal venues for tea with home made shortbread, a wee dram or just to relax and gaze out to sea. The five bedrooms in the former Campbell family home, which is the main building, have Kingsize beds, two being designated Junior Suite and Master Bedroom. Dining in the AA two Rosette Asknish Bay Restaurant is another experience to savour. Choose from freshly caught langoustine, lobster and crab, Islay scallops, select meat and game from nearby Aird Farm and fresh vegetables and herbs, all sourced locally. A less formal option is available in the Chartroom II Bistro, which has high chairs and a childrens' menu available. Staying here is an unforgettable experience.

DINING: Table d'hôte 4 courses £39.50pp. Evening meals from 1830, Last orders 2045. Breakfast is from 0800.

BEDROOMS: 25
All 25 bedrooms have stunning views out over Asknish Bay towards the islands of Jura, Shuna and Scarba. Five of the bedrooms in the Canadian Lodge style annexe have been designated Superior with extra touches of luxury to make your stay special. Ten of the annexe bedrooms are on the ground floor.

B&B PER ROOM PER NIGHT:
D: £150.00 - £312.00

ADDITIONAL INFORMATION:
Visit Scotland Gold Award. Open all year apart from last three weeks in January. Gourmet Nights four times a year.

Site: ✿ P **Payment:** 💳 **Leisure:** 🚲 ♪ ▶ ☉ **Property:** 🍴 🐾 🖃 🖥 🅿 🔌 **Children:** 🚼 🛏 🚼
Catering: (✕ ⚓ ♨ **Room:** 🍵 🍷 📞 TV DVD

BLACKADDIE COUNTRY HOUSE HOTEL

BEDROOMS: 7
Seven bedrooms and suites and two self contained cottages in grounds each with fully fitted kitchen.

B&B PER ROOM PER NIGHT:
S: £80.00 - £155.00
D: £95.00 - £175.00

ADDITIONAL INFORMATION:
Suite from £180. 2 nights dinner, b&b from £85.00 pppn; 3 nights from £78.00 pppn; 4+ nights from £70.00 pppn. Gourmet menu & breaks available. Birdwatching, shooting, biking, walking, fishing and swimming nearby. Open all year. Glasgow 45 miles and Edinburgh 70 miles.

Blackaddie Road, Sanquhar, Dumfries and Galloway, Scotland DG4 6JJ
T: (01659) 50270 **F:** (01659) 495935
E: ian@blackaddiehotel.co.uk **W:** www.blackaddiehotel.co.uk

A superb small hotel set in its own gardens on the banks of the river Nith, one of Scotland's great yet little known salmon rivers and with extensive views across Scotland's Southern Upland Way. Seven beautiful bedrooms and suites, many of which overlook the gardens or the river some with stunning bathrooms. There are also two self-contained cottages in the grounds, each with fully fitted kitchen, for those who wish to be independent. But who would when the hotel boasts food to rival the best anywhere! It is far and away above what one would expect in a small tucked away country house hotel. Chef/Proprietor Ian McAndrew has held a Michelin star for many years in previous restaurants and his menus use fresh local produce with all dishes prepared daily on the premises, now offering two menus; a 4 course fine dining menu and a 7 course Gourmet tasting menu both of which change daily. Dumfries House and Drumlanrig Castle within a short drive with Caerlaverock and Threave castles nearby.

DINING: 2 AA Rosettes. Gourmet menu; lunch & special diets available. Last orders 2100. Breakfast from 0730.

Site: ❀ P Payment: 💳 Leisure: ♪ ↾ Property: ⚡ 🐾 ⛩ Room: ⓐ 📺 📀 🎧 🛏

EDDRACHILLES HOTEL

Badcall Bay, Scourie, The Highlands, Scotland IV27 4TH
T: (01971) 502080 **F:** (01971) 502477
E: info@eddrachilles.com **W:** www.eddrachilles.com

Presbyterian ministers had a knack of choosing perfect sites for their Manses and Eddrachilles is no exception. Sheltered by gentle hills and with stunning views, this is a place to escape to. The owners are enthusiastic about their home and enjoy sharing it with their guests. The North of Scotland is unique. Its remote and untouched beauty can be best explored on quiet single track roads, or by one of the numerous scenic walks and climbs over beach, cliff and hill, many starting directly from the hotel. Handa Island, the famous bird sanctuary, can easily be visited by boat from nearby Tarbet. There is no restriction on the number of brown trout which may be caught on nearby hill lochs.

DINING: Last orders for dinner 2000; bar lunches & special diets available. Everything is home produced with a selection of home-smoked produce and homemade charcuterie. The menu changes daily with a wine list of over 70 bins and over 140 malt whiskies. The seafood is outstanding and the beef, venison and lamb from Highland farms unsurpassed. The restaurant is now located in the conservatory with outstanding views over the islands.

BEDROOMS: 11
Every bedroom has private en suite facilities, direct dial telephone and Wi-Fi. There is also ironing facilities, hairdryer and a trouser press in each room, along with a colour television, radio, tea and coffee making facilities.

B&B PER ROOM PER NIGHT:
S: £80.00
D: £110.00

ADDITIONAL INFORMATION:
Open April 1st - October 1st.

Site: ❀ P Payment: 💷 Leisure: ♪ Property: 🖥 Catering: (✕ 🍷 Room: 🗗 ♨ 📞 📺 📧 🧴

VIEWFIELD HOUSE

BEDROOMS: 10

The 10 en suite bedrooms have been tastefully decorated, each in their own style, with several overlooking the bay.

B&B PER ROOM PER NIGHT:
S: £64.00 - £77.00
D: £128.00 - £150.00

ADDITIONAL INFORMATION:
There is one ground floor wheelchair accessible room available. Viewfield House is open April - October.

Portree, Isle of Skye, Scotland IV51 9EU
T: (01478) 612217 **F:** (01478) 613517
E: info@viewfieldhouse.com **W:** www.viewfieldhouse.com

Viewfield House standing in extensive wooded grounds on the outskirts of Portree, overlooking Portree Bay and within easy walking distance of the centre, has been the home of the Macdonald family for over 200 years. The house is full of character and charm and has retained many of its Victorian features. There is plenty to do on Skye; boat trips, fishing, sailing, walking in the Cuillin hills, pony trekking and golf. Visit the otter haven at Kylerhea or visit Dunvegan Castle, home to the MacLeod clan since time immemorial. After an invigorating day your host Hugh Macdonald can offer dinner, by prior arrangement, or can recommend several eateries in the nearby town of Portree. Activities nearby include sailing, squash, shooting and indoor pool all within 1 mile. Fishing 2 miles, riding 3 miles, golf 9 miles.

DINING: Table d'hôte 3 course dinner ca £25 available by prior arrangement and served from 1900 with the last sitting at 2030. Cooked breakfast from 0800.

Site: ❀ P Payment: 💳 Leisure: ♪ ▶ Property: ☂ 🛏 Catering: ✖ Room: 🍵 ♨ 📺 📀

DUISDALE HOUSE HOTEL

Isle Ornsay, Sleat, Isle of Skye IV43 8QW
T: (01471) 833202
E: info@duisdale.com **W:** www.duisdale.com

Situated in the area known as Sleat on the southernmost tip of Skye, this Hebridean hotel was built in 1865 as a Hunting Lodge set within 35 acres of beautiful mature gardens. It has been completely transformed by owners Anne Gracie and Captain Ken Gunn into a peaceful retreat. The restaurant presents the diner with choice before you even see a menu – will you choose to dine in the fine dining restaurant, with two AA rosettes, or in the less formal Chart Room offering an à la carte menu? Whichever you choose, the setting will provide the perfect ambience in which to savour the innovative dishes created daily by the hotel's kitchen team. The award winning restaurant and exclusive daily sailing trips from April to September on board the hotel's luxury yacht, skippered by Ken, add a whole new dimension to a short break on the Isle of Skye.

DINING: 2 AA Rosette. À la carte 3 courses, £35pp; table d'hôte £49pp.

BEDROOMS: 18
18 individually designed bedrooms of varying sizes and room types, in a range of contemporary styles.

B&B PER ROOM PER NIGHT:
S: £79.00
D: £99.00

ADDITIONAL INFORMATION:
VisitScotland Scottish Thistle Award Winner - Best Hotel. This peaceful, romantic hotel is an ideal base for exploring Skye, whether from the land or the sea. The nearby Toravaig House Hotel is under the same ownership.

Open all year.

Site: ❀ P **Payment:** 💳 **Leisure:** ♪ **Property:** 🔥 🐾 🖼 🗄 🏠 🌳 **Children:** 🍼 🛏 🎠 **Catering:** 🍴 🍽 🍺 **Room:** 🍵 🛁 📞 📺 📀 🎧 🖨

TORAVAIG HOUSE HOTEL

BEDROOMS: 9
All of the nine individually designed rooms are intimate in character and rich in fabrics and contemporary furnishings.

B&B PER ROOM PER NIGHT:
S: £79.00
D: £99.00

ADDITIONAL INFORMATION:
Open all year.

Sleat, Isle of Skye IV44 8RE
T: (01471) 820 200
E: info@skyehotel.co.uk W: www.skyehotel.co.uk

Toravaig House Hotel, on the Isle of Skye, Scotland is a small, contemporary Hebridean Gem. The hotel's peaceful location with views over the ruins of Knock Castle c.1345 and the Sound of Sleat is the perfect place to relax and unwind. The lounge offers stylish sofas and a crackling log fire, perfect for enjoying fine malts or delicious wines before dinner where the finest modern cuisine is served. All ingredients are locally sourced from Skye and around Scotland, from the freshly caught langoustines and lobsters to home grown leaves and herbs. This small, romantic, island hotel is the result of a long held dream of owners, Anne Gracie and Captain Ken Gunn, to create an intimate boutique hotel on their home island of Skye. It offers a unique combination of comfort, fine dining, and the opportunity to join them on their 50' yacht 'Solus a Chuain' (Light of the Ocean) skippered by Ken, for daily summer sailing trips around Skye. The nearby Duisdale House Hotel is under the same ownership.

DINING: 2 AA Rosette dining. À la carte, 3 courses £30pp; Fine dining -5 courses £47pp.

Site: **Payment:** **Leisure:** **Property:** **Children:** **Catering:**
Room:

THE WINNOCK HOTEL

The Square, Drymen, Loch Lomond G63 0BL
T: (01360) 660245
E: info@winnockhotel.com **W:** www.winnockhotel.com

Picture yourself soaking up the atmosphere of this 18th century Inn near Loch Lomond, sitting beside the roaring log fire whilst planning your day's exploration of the surrounding beautiful Trossachs countryside with many castles, gardens and city attractions within easy reach. After a full day's excitement, return to your tasteful Elegance or Heritage bedroom, many with balconies or four poster beds, to prepare for a night to remember; good food, fine wine and friendly service. The Winnock Hotel has a variety of wining and dining options available for guests. Choose from the historic and intimate Merlin Restaurant, the characterful and cozy Ptarmigan Bar or the popular Capercaillie Room where entertaining evenings abound! Situated just three miles from Loch Lomond, the hotel is ideally placed in the golden triangle between Edinburgh, Glasgow and Stirling. Drive time from Glasgow and Stirling is 30 minutes and 1 hour from Edinburgh. The Winnock is also a great first stop for anyone tackling the West Highland Way.

DINING: Table d'hôte menu priced at £18.50pp and a Taste of Scotland menu at £26.50, as well as à la carte dishes. The restaurant is open 7 days, between 1800 – 2130.
Site: P Payment: 💷 **Leisure:** 🎿 ♪ ⏲ ☂ **Property:** 🍴 📺 🖥 🔌 🌙 ⊘ **Children:** 👶 🛏 🚼
Catering: 🍴✕ ⏲ 🍽 **Room:** 🍵 ✦ 📞 📷 📺 📠

BEDROOMS: 73
Elegance or Heritage bedrooms available, many with balconies or four poster beds.

B&B PER ROOM PER NIGHT:
S: £79.00 - £119.00
D: £138.00 - £168.00

ADDITIONAL INFORMATION:
Open all year.

The bar serves everything from homemade pies, burgers, fish to sirloin steaks. Meals served here between 1200 – 2130.

THE FOUR SEASONS HOTEL

BEDROOMS: 18
Twelve bedrooms and, in the grounds, six chalets, ideal for families, and a holiday apartment.

B&B PER ROOM PER NIGHT:
S: £57.00
D: £114.00

ADDITIONAL INFORMATION:
Four for three, three for two, romantic, wine tasting, walking, art, Christmas and Hogmanay breaks available.

The Four Seasons hotel is open March - December; weekends only in March, November & December.

St Fillans, Perthshire, Scotland PH6 2NF
T: (01764) 685333 **F:** (01764) 685444
E: info@thefourseasonshotel.co.uk **W:** www.thefourseasonshotel.co.uk

The Four Seasons sits in glorious countryside on the banks of Loch Earn. The hotel faces south-west down the loch, the view changing with the seasons: fresh, new colours in spring, long, light summer evenings with spectacular sunsets, morning mists in autumn and snow covered Munros in Winter. Originally built in the early 19th century for the manager of the lime kilns, the main house then became the schoolmaster's house. Converted in the 1900s, it has been extended over the years into the comfortable hotel it now is. Upstairs there is a small comfy library which has books for every taste and a collection of CDs. Two AA rosette dining either being in the Meall Reamhar (High Hills) Restaurant, specialising in local produce, or in the less formal Tarken room. The hotel has its own jetty and there is a 9-hole golf course in the village. The Four Seasons provides a wonderful base from which to explore Perthshire and the Heart of Scotland.

DINING: 2 AA Rosette dining in either the fine dining Meall Reamhar Restaurant or less formal Tarken Bistro. Served until 2100.

Site: ✿ P Payment: 💳 Leisure: ♪ ▶ Property: 🔥 🐕 🖥 ♨ ∅ Children: 🛏 🎠 🎎 Catering: (✗ 🍷 🍽 Room: 🗝 💧 📞 📺 📀 🎬 🍴

MURRAYSHALL HOTEL & GOLF COURSES

Scone, Perth, Scotland PH2 7PH
T: (01738) 551171 **F:** (01738)552595
E: sales@murrayshall.co.uk **W:** www.murrayshall.co.uk

Murrayshall House Hotel sits in grounds of some 350 acres, just a few miles from the city of Perth, and with excellent views over the surrounding countryside. The AA two Rosette Old Masters restaurant provides the opportunity for some excellent Scottish produce – how about some Isle of Lewis mussels to start with, followed by a Forfar rack of lamb with confit shoulder, and then toasted maple marshmallow or Perthshire ice creams to finish? More informal dining options are available in the Clubhouse, and for small groups private dining rooms can be arranged. For golfing fans, the hotel has not one but two golf courses: the Murrayshall championship course (6400 yards and par 73) and the slightly shorter Lyndoch course (5400 yards and par 69). But what if you are not a golfer? Perth is situated very centrally in Scotland, so a wide range of tours and excursions can be made, using Murrayshall as a base - Edinburgh, Glasgow, St Andrews, the Highlands, Royal Deeside and much more, all waiting to be explored.

DINING: AA 2 Rosette Old Masters Restaurant, informal dining in the clubhouse.

BEDROOMS: 41
There are 41 bedrooms and suites to choose from, with all the facilities the business or leisure traveller would expect.

B&B PER ROOM PER NIGHT:
S: £80.00 - £110.00
D: £80.00 - £160.00

ADDITIONAL INFORMATION:
Open all year.

Site: ❀ P **Payment:** 💳 **Leisure:** 🎣 🏌 ⚲ **Property:** 🍴 🐕 🖼 🗄 ♨ ⌀ **Children:** 🛝 🛏 ⚘
Catering: 🍴✗ 🍷 🍳 **Room:** 🧺 📶 ☎ 📷 ⎙

ATHOLL PALACE HOTEL, SPA & LODGES

BEDROOMS: 90
Singles through family suites and four posters to Turret rooms, Highland Lodges in the grounds, cottages, self-catering apartments and an 8 bed Manor House.

B&B PER ROOM PER NIGHT:
S: £85.00 - £265.00
D: £115.00 - £295.00

ADDITIONAL INFORMATION:
Countryside setting with walking, shooting, watersports and fishing nearby.

Open all year.

Pitlochry, Perthshire, Scotland PH16 5LY
T: (01796) 472400 **F:** (01796) 473036
E: gillian@athollpalace.com **W:** www.athollpalace.com

The Atholl Palace, a stunning Victorian hotel, towers above Pitlochry, the tourist capital of the Highlands, with beautiful views on all sides. It started life as a Hydropathic Establishment whose history is chronicled in its own museum. Refurbished bedrooms range from singles through family suites and four posters to Turret rooms (ideal for honeymooners) and Highland Lodges in the grounds, cottages, self-catering apartments and the Manor House. Recently an 8-bedroom manor house has also become available. Close by there are endless things to do and see. Sports include golf, tennis, fishing, walking, mountain biking, pony trekking, kayaking and pitch'n putt. Other local attractions include the amazing 'salmon ladder', historic Blair Castle (with the only private army in the British Isles), the House of Bruar – the 'Harrods of the North' – the shops of Pitlochry and the renowned Festival Theatre. In the evening, return to the hotel to enjoy a drink in the bar, and dine in the Verandah Restaurant with its growing reputation for quality food making best use of local produce.

DINING: 3 course table d'hôte dinner; à la carte, lunch & special diets; until 2100; breakfast from 0730.
Site: ⚘ P **Payment:** 🖃 **Leisure:** ♿ ⛏ 🏊 🎣 ⚲ ⚲ **Property:** 🌳 **Children:** 👶 **Catering:** ⟨✕ 🍴 **Room:** ♿ 📠

ROMAN CAMP COUNTRY HOUSE HOTEL & RESTAURANT

Main Street, Callander, Stirling, Scotland FK17 8BG
T: (01877) 330003 **F:** (01877) 331533
E: mail@romancamphotel.co.uk **W:** www.romancamphotel.co.uk

The Roman Camp Country House & Restaurant lies on 20 acres of gardens by the river Teith. These include a large walled flower & herb garden and rolling lawns. The house, dating from 1625, was originally a hunting lodge for the Dukes of Perth and was converted to a hotel in 1939, the Brown family have run the property since 1989. Public rooms are exceptionally comfortable, with deep sofas and armchairs, roaring fires in winter and fresh flowers. In the heart of the house is the library with its rich oak panelling and adjoining secret chapel. The AA 3 Rosette restaurant is an inspiring oval room of elegant proportions, with soft modern classical décor. Cuisine is modern Scottish making use of freshest local produce. There is a smaller private dining room for special occasions or private parties. Weddings and small conferences can also be catered for. Callander is in the Loch Lomond and Trossachs National Park, in Rob Roy country yet conveniently situated for Stirling and just over an hour from both Glasgow and Edinburgh. Pets are welcome - no charge.

DINING: 4 course table d'hôte dinner £55. À la carte, lunch & special diets available. Last orders 2100; breakfast from 0745.

BEDROOMS: 15
Each bedroom is individually furnished with rich fabrics and antiques, many being on the ground floor.

B&B PER ROOM PER NIGHT:
S: £110.00
D: £160.00

ADDITIONAL INFORMATION:
Low season midweek breaks – 2 nights dinner, b&b from £396 per room.

Site: ❀ P Leisure: ♪ ▶ Property: 🛋 🐴 🖥 🔲 Children: ⚲ Room: ♨

WALES

Wales is a land of beautiful coastline, lakes and forests, hidden valleys and high mountains. It has three National Parks in Snowdonia, the Pembrokeshire Coast and the Brecon Beacons, several official Areas of Outstanding Natural Beauty and long stretches of protected Heritage Coast, not to mention its own language, traditions, music and culture. From the fine beaches and seaside towns of the north, through mid wales with its rich, scenic landscape, coastal walks and castles, to the cultural capital and heritage trails of the south, every corner of Wales has something new to discover. Croeso means Welcome and you will hear it often.

WALES

NORTH WALES

North Wales has been attracting holiday visitors for over two hundred years with some of the best scenery in the world. There is a wide choice that includes the Snowdonia National Park, the Llŷn Peninsula and Cambrian Coastline, castles, narrow-gauge railways, golf, cycling, walking, award winning beaches, country parks, World Heritage Sites and Areas of Outstanding Natural Beauty. Llandudno is a beautiful Victorian seaside resort at the foot of the Great Orme and nearby the peaceful Carneddau is one hundred square miles of beautiful mountain moorland, dotted with Neolithic tracks, standing stones, Bronze Age sites and beautiful lakes.

This is very much a place for rural pleasures. The Hiraethog Mountains in the north east, The Berwyns south of Llangollen and the beautiful river valleys of the Conwy, Clwyd, Dee and Glaslyn have a magic all of their own. The views from the top of Moel Famau, the highest peak in the Clwydian Range, are stunning with Merseyside, Snowdonia and the Dee Valley all laid out before you. Snowdonia is justly famous for its 823 square miles of national park with magnificent mountains, lakes, forests and the Snowdon Mountain Railway, one of the The Great Little Trains of Wales. Mount Snowdon is the highest in Wales at 3,560 ft and Cadair Idris, near Dolgellau, is one of the most popular.

Erddig
Wrexham LL13 0YT
(01978) 355314
www.nationaltrust.org.uk/erddig
Widely acclaimed as one of Britain's finest historic houses, Erddig is a fascinating early 18th-century country house set in a superb formal garden and romantic landscape park.

North Wales is also home to some of the most spectacular drives in the British Isles. The road from Dolgellau to Tal-y-Lynn has heartstopping views or try Trawsfynydd via Llyn Celyn Lake to Bala for incredible scenery. Swallow Falls, or Rhaeadr Ewynnol to give it its proper Welsh name, is a spectacular waterfall on the A5 between Betws-y-Coed and Capel Curig and a must see for its sheer beauty.

Wrexham is the region's biggest town with nearby attractions including the splendid Erddig country house and several museums dedicated to the area's lead, coal and iron heritage. The pretty market town of Llangollen is a great holiday base, with the Llangollen Canal, Horseshoe Falls, Valle Crucis Abbey and Dinas Bran Castle all within walking distance of the town. Discover the wildlife of the Dee Estuary on the Alwen Trail, enjoy quiet riversides in Flintshire or forests and lakes in the Conwy Valley – there's more than enough space for a good ramble.

The 12th and 13th century Welsh castles were masterpieces of military architecture. Conwy, Caernarvon and Beaumaris are breathtaking in their size and splendour, while the keeps of Dolwyddelan and Dolbadarn will appeal to romantics. Chirk Castle is one of Edward I's 'ring of steel' fortresses and has the area's best formal gardens. Medieval towns such as Ruthin, splendid Jacobean farmhouses, fine Elizabethan houses, workers cottages and the slate caverns of Blaenau Ffestiniog, Glyn Ceiriog and Llanberis show the different sides of life in this historic region and can all be visited today.

MID WALES

Mid Wales is a land of dramatic contrasts where the pleasures of coast and countryside can be equally enjoyed. This is a region of immense natural beauty boasting much of the Snowdonia National Park, a coastline dotted with small fishing villages and popular seaside resorts, as well as sandy beaches, rugged cliffs and secluded coves.

The Centre for Alternative Technology
Machynlleth, Powys SY20 9AZ,
(01654) 705950 • www.cat.org.uk
Over 40 years pioneering new energy technologies to tackle climate change and diversify energy supplies, plus an amazingly steep water-balanced cliff railway.

Rural life is centred around a series of small towns, linked by splendid mountain roads or old drovers' ways. Pretty Llanidoes, with its 16th century market hall, stands almost at the centre of Wales at the confluence of the Severn and Clywedog rivers. Historic Machynlleth is where the Welsh rebel leader Owain Glyndwr set up his Welsh Parliament in 1404 and today it has a number of visitor attractions including MOMA, Wales (Museum Of Modern Art).

To the east, the Welsh Marches with their traditional black and white buildings were once governed by the Marcher Lords on behalf of the King. Significant traces of the massive dyke, built by the 8th century Saxon king to keep marauding Welsh forces out of his kingdom, remain forming the basis of Offa's Dyke Trail, a 168 mile north to south walkway. Charming, lively market towns jostle for attention, with literary and outdoorsy types well catered for. Stop for lunch and book shopping in Hay-on-Wye, regarded as the second-hand book capital of the world. A year-round programme of festivals and cultural events is also on offer including the Hay Festival and HowTheLightGetsIn.

The Brecon Beacons National Park includes majestic reservoirs, waterfalls and caves and is perfect for walking and horseriding, particularly around the Black Mountains, where both novice and experienced riders will find fabulous trekking. The Beacons Way is a magical 152km (95mile) walk across the Park. From gentle cycling between pretty villages to extreme mountain biking, the Beacons has something for every pedalling style and also has one of Europe's longest cave networks. Don't miss the awe-inspiring architecture of Brecon Cathedral or the annual summer Brecon Jazz festival, both of which draw visitors from far and wide.

Ceredigion and Cardigan Bay have a multitude of attractions for visitors, indoor and out. The award-winning Aberystwyth Arts Centre is Wales' largest, with a wide-ranging artistic programme of drama, dance, music and visual arts. The Cambrian Mountains, Wales' backbone, is an upland region where hamlets and farms nestle in the folds of endless hills. One of the most beautiful sights is Devil's Bridge spanning the Mynach River. Mid Wales has always had a seafaring tradition - schooners used to set out from the little ports of Aberaeron, Aberdovey, Aberystwyth and New Quay, which today bustle with pleasure craft. The Wales Coast Path, ideal for novice and expert hikers alike, traces the entire shoreline of this region all the way down to Cardigan, the gateway to the picturesque Teifi Valley.

WEST WALES

At 186 miles long and guarded on its western rim by Britain's smallest city, St David's, the rugged Pembrokeshire Coastal Path offers sweeping cliff tops, secret coves, estuaries and wide sandy beaches. The Pembrokeshire Coast National Park has moorlands rising gently to the Preseli Hills, while Stone Age forts and Norman castles reflect the area's ancient history. St David's Cathedral was founded by the eponymous saint in the 8th century and is still in use today.

Camarthenshire brings stories to life, from the intriguing mythology of Merlin to the gritty wildboy poetry of Dylan Thomas. Stretching from Carmarthen Bay in the south to the western Brecon Beacons in the north, think lush rural landscapes, crystalline coastlines and the rugged foothills of the Brecon Beacons National Park. You'll find chic places to stay, stylish eateries, great local produce and welcoming country pubs. There's plenty of history here too. Near Carmarthen is Dylan Thomas' village of Laugharne, in whose churchyard he is buried. Up country the Dolaucothi gold mines, started by the Romans, are now a museum. Kidwelly Castle is on a par with other great castles of Wales and the National Wool Museum tells the story of an important industry. Carmarthenshire is also home to some of Wales' longest beaches - heaven for swimmers, beachcombers, walkers, wildlife-watchers and other outdoor adventures.

National Botanic Garden of Wales
Carmarthenshire SA32 8HG
(01558) 668768
www.gardenofwales.org.uk
A world-class visitor attraction and centre for botanical research and conservation. Set in 568 acres of beautiful countryside, it features the world's largest single-span glasshouse.

Sitting on the 5 mile sweep of Swansea Bay, Wales' second city enjoys a location that is hard to beat with most city centre attractions and shops only a short walk from the sea. At the National Waterfront Museum take in the sights and sounds of more than 300 years of Welsh industry and innovation. The Dylan Thomas Centre celebrates Swansea's famous son with a permanent exhibition on Dylan and his life, housed in a splendid listed building.

Follow the coast and you'll reach the UK's first Area of Outstanding Natural Beauty, the Gower Peninsula. A secluded world of its own, with limestone cliffs, remote bays and miles of golden sands, the Peninsula is Wales' very own 'Riviera'. Historic sites not to be missed include 13th century Weobley Castle, the ruins of Threecliff Bay and Gower Farm Museum with its 100 year old farm memorabilia. Outside Port Talbot, the 850 acre Margam Country Park includes an Iron Age hill fort, a restored abbey church with windows by William Morris, Margam Stones Museum with stones and crosses dating form the 5th-11th centuries and the main house with its 327ft orangery. En route to Cardiff are the late 19th century Castell Coch (Red Castle), a mixture of Victorian Gothic and fairytale styles and the well preserved 13th century Caerphilly Castle, with its famous leaning tower.

Cardiff Castle 🖼
Cardiff CF10 3RB
(029) 2087 8100
www.cardiffcastle.com
In the heart of the capital, Cardiff Castle's enchanting fairytale towers conceal an elaborate and splendid interior. Climb up to the top of the 12th century Norman keep for great views over the city.

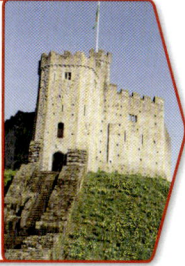

SOUTH WALES

Think of green valleys, warm welcomes, castles, myths and magic. Think of a unique industrial heritage, male voice choirs and stunning scenery. If you want a real Welsh experience then you must visit South Wales. The Vale of Glamorgan is perfect for those who love the outdoor life and discovering towns and villages packed full of traditional charm and character. Porthcawl and Barry Island are cheerful beach holiday resorts fringed by the striking Heritage Coast and lovely green countryside. The remains of the Norman Ogmore Castle can be found beside the river Ewenny, the joining point of two major Welsh counties of Bridgend and the Vale of Glamorgan. A few miles west of Cardiff, in the heart of the Vale of Glamorgan countryside, Dyffryn Gardens has over 55 acres of exceptional Edwardian garden design and is easily one of the most beautiful gardens in Wales.

Cardiff is Wales' capital city and at its heart, the spectacular castle walls conceal a fascinating history. Modern Cardiff offers spectacular shopping, museums, dining and entertainment - be sure to visit the free National Museum Cardiff. Cyfarthfa Castle built in 1824, is an impressive homage to the Industrial Revolution and a great day out. Take a ride on a vintage steam locomotive through beautiful scenery along the length of the Taf Fechan Reservoir to Torpantau, high in the Brecon Beacons, on one of the

most popular railways in Wales. Blaenavon is one of the best preserved 18th century ironworks in Europe, complete with furnaces, cast houses, a magnificent water balance tower, calcining kilns and ironworkers cottages. High on the bracken-covered moors of north Gwent near Blaenavon, Big Pit, now the National Mining Museum of Wales, is part of the Blaenavon World Heritage Site.

The borderlands of the Wye Valley and Vale of Usk, once home to King Arthur, the Romans and the Normans, today offer a wealth of heritage, dramatic landscapes, nature trails, walking, mountain biking and canoeing, as well as great food. Wales' boundary with England is marked by the Black Mountains, north of Abergavenny, rising to 2,660 feet at Waun Fach. Hay Bluff, near Llanthony Priory affords amazing views westwards. Great castles are the legacy of Llywelyn the Great's resistance to the English and ancient monastic orders sought solitude at settlements such as Tintern Abbey. Usk's charm lies in its riverside walks and small independent shops, tearooms and pubs, and it hosts a fantastic Winter Festival. The remains of Caerleon Roman Fortress and Baths near Newport paint a vivid picture of life in second-century Roman Britain, while the Offa's Dyke National Trail is just one of the borderlands many long distance footpaths. In the Welsh section of The Wye Valley Area of Outstanding Natural Beauty, the A466 is a beautiful valley road that winds along the gorge from Chepstow to Monmouth, perfect for a leisurely drive.

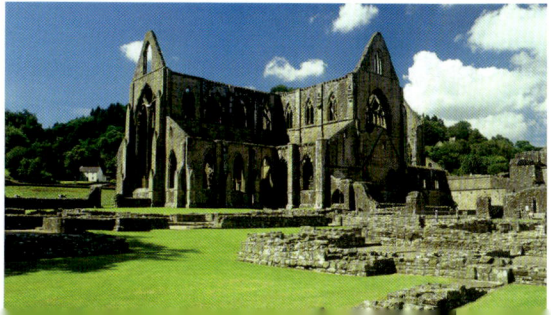

HUDSON'S HISTORIC HOUSES & GARDENS HIGHLIGHTS

Aberglasney Gardens
(01558) 668998
www.aberglasney.org
Aberglasney is one of Wales' finest gardens - a renowed plantsman's paradise of more than 10 acres with a unique Elizabethan cloister garden at its heart.

Fonmon Castle
(01446) 710206
www.fonmoncastle.com
Fonmon is one of few medieval castles still lived in as a home, since being built c1200. Take the guided tour through the fascinating history of the Castle, its families, architecture and interiors.

Gregynog
(01686) 650224
www.gregynog.org
Grade 1 listed gardens, historic oak panelled rooms, an extensive library and a fine collection of furniture.

Gwydir Castle
(01492) 641687
www.gwydircastle.co.uk
Situated in the beautiful Conwy Valley and is set within a Grade I listed, 10 acre garden. Gwydir is a fine example of a Tudor courtyard house, incorporating re-used medieval material from the dissolved Abbey of Maenan.

The Hall at Abbey Cwm Hir
(01597) 851727
www.abbeycwmhir.com
It is one of Wales' finest examples of Victorian Gothic Revival archiecture, and is surrounded by beautiful and noteable 12 acre gardens.

Llanvihangel Court
(01873) 890217
www.llanvihangelcourt.com
Grade 1 Tudor Manor with fine hall, unusual yew staircase and many 17th century moulded plaster ceilings.

Penrhyn Castle
(01248) 353084
www.nationaltrust.org.uk
Discover opulence on a grand scale and enjoy spectacular views of Snowdonia and the sea. Extensive parkland and gardens offer great walks.

Plas Newydd House and Gardens
(01248) 714795
www.nationaltrust.org.uk/plasnewydd
This elegant house is famed for its fascinating fantasy mural by the artist Rex Whistler.

Powis Castle
(01938) 551944
www.nationaltrust.org.uk/powis-castle
Powis Castle has been transformed over 400 years from a stark medieval fortress to an extravagant family home.

HUDSON'S
HISTORIC HOUSES & GARDENS
MUSEUMS & HERITAGE SITES

For more suggestions of great historic days out across Britain visit
www.hudsonsheritage.com

WALES
WHERE TO STAY

Entries appear alphabetically by town name in each county.
A key to symbols appears on page 4.

NANTEOS MANSION

Rhydyfelin, Aberystwyth, Ceredigion SY23 4LU
T: (01970) 600522
E: info@nanteos.com **W:** www.nanteos.com

Nanteos Mansion is a perfect blend of old and new, laid out across this historic Grade I Listed Georgian mansion, its adjoining former bakery and Palladian carriage house. The mansion is unveiled at the end of a mile-long drive, with a small lake, walled garden and 25 acres of ancient woodland. Views take in nearby hills, four pillars stand sentinel at the front door, sofas by log fires await in the hall. The house dates back to 1731 but has medieval foundations. It is most famous for the Nanteos Cup – The Holy Grail – which, legend says, was borne here by the monks of Glastonbury Abbey during the Dissolution of the Monasteries. A magnificent renovation has brought the house back to vibrant life. Downstairs there's a morning room, sitting room bar and elegant Nightingale Restaurant where you can sample chef/patron Nigel Jones' delicious cuisine. Upstairs suites are grand and gracious, some panelled, others with fine wallpaper. The luxury rooms burst with colour and original art.

DINING: Brunch* 1100-1400. Afternoon Tea 1400-1630. Dinner 1830-2100. *Brunch on Saturdays is by booking only.

BEDROOMS: 14
Luxury accommodation is provided by 14 well appointed, individually designed, luxury en suite bedrooms, together with a magnificent four-bedroom Mews House.

B&B PER ROOM PER NIGHT:
D: £125.00 - £300.00

ADDITIONAL INFORMATION:
Open all year. Watersports, riding, golf, superb walks, Rheidol Steam Railway and the Mynach Falls are all nearby. Licensed for weddings.

Site: ✿ P **Payment:** 💳 **Leisure:** ♪ ↑ ∪ ⚙ **Property:** ⚑ 🐾 ⌨ 🎵 ◑ ⌀ **Children:** 🚲 🛏 🎃
Catering: (✕ ♟ 🍽 **Room:** 🔲 ☕ 📺 📀 ⚿

THE FALCONDALE HOTEL AND RESTAURANT

BEDROOMS: 19
All rooms en suite, warm and comfortable with fluffy bathrobes, towels and amenities. Flat-screen TV's/DVD. Best rooms include one with a four-poster bed and Juliet balcony, another with a super king size bed and window seat.

B&B PER ROOM PER NIGHT:
D: £100.00 - £190.00

ADDITIONAL INFORMATION:
Open all year. Doubles from £100 to £190 per room per night bed and breakfast. Dinner bed and breakfast from £180 per room per night - based on two people sharing.

Falcondale Drive, Lampeter, Ceredigion SA48 7RX
T: (01570) 422910 **F:** (01570) 422910
E: info@thefalcondale.co.uk **W:** www.thefalcondale.co.uk

The Falcondale hotel and two AA Rosette restaurant near the University town of Lampeter is only 30 minutes from the coastal villages of Cardigan Bay and hilly, marshy regions of the Cambrian Mountains. A wealth of walking, cycling, fishing, and open gardens are within easy reach of this Central Wales location. Why not visit the local National Trust properties before sinking into a warm, comfy sofa in the lounge with a glass, or two, of wine from the extensive list? Follow this with lunch or dinner prepared by Dafydd Davies' team using only the best of ingredients from Ceredigion, Carmarthen and surrounding counties in Mid Wales. If you do not have time for lunch or dinner, drop in for a coffee and read the newspaper in the lounge, in the heated conservatory or on the terrace that overlooks the Teifi valley towards Lampeter. Scrumptious homemade cakes with a pot of Earl Grey are also ideal, come rain or shine.

DINING: Full à la carte dinner menu served from 1830 - 2030 at £40 per person for three courses with canapes.

Site: ✿ **P Payment:** 💳 **Leisure:** ♪ **Property:** 🐕 🏡 **Children:** 🍼 🛏 ♿ **Catering:** 🍴 ♟ **Room:** ☎ 📺 📀

ST TUDNO HOTEL

Promenade, Llandudno, Conwy LL30 2LP
T: (01492) 874411 **F:** (01492) 860407
E: sttudnohotel@btinternet.com **W:** www.st-tudno.co.uk

Situated at the far end of Llandudno's fine promenade, opposite the pier, St Tudno is one of Wales' leading hotels and has won many prestigious awards. The charming and efficient staff make guests feel instantly at home. The Terrace Restaurant has outstanding murals of Lake Como and Italian-style decor. Chef Andrew Foster has built the restaurant's reputation up to being one of the best in Wales, with plaudits from Clarissa Dickson-Wright and Bill Bryson, among others. Excellent bar meals are also available at lunchtime and the number of locals who rendezvous for this is evidence of their popularity. The Terrace Restaurant holds two AA Rosettes, which also serve Award Winning Afternoon Teas. The lounges have a Victorian theme with comfortable chairs and restful colours. Alice Liddell, better known as Lewis Carroll's Alice in Wonderland, stayed here at the age of 8. St Tudno is ideally situated for visits to Snowdonia, Conwy & Caernarfon Castles and Bodnant Gardens.

DINING: À la carte dinner Terrace Restaurant; lunch & special diets available; last orders 2130; breakfast from 0730.

Site: P Payment: ⌨ **Leisure:** ▶ **Property:** 🐾 🖼 ⚕ **Children:** 🍼 ⛺ ♿ **Catering:** (✕ ⛄ 🍽
Room: 🔌 ✦ 📞 📺 🧺

BEDROOMS: 18
Bedrooms are individually decorated & include 2 suites. Special touches include Molton Brown toiletries & bathrobes.

B&B PER ROOM PER NIGHT:
S: £80.00 - £90.00
D: £104.00 - £310.00

ADDITIONAL INFORMATION:
Winter Special Offers per room per night min stay of 2 nights Dinner, Bed & Breakfast from £145.00 per night. For up to date special offers please visit our website.

FFIN Y PARC COUNTRY HOUSE

BEDROOMS: 6
Rooms are sophisticated and unique, with a mixture of antique and contemporary furnishings and original art. All the rooms have en suite bathrooms, superking beds, flat screen TV and panoramic views of the Conwy Valley.

B&B PER ROOM PER NIGHT:
S: £125.00 - £190.00
D: £145.00 - £210.00

ADDITIONAL INFORMATION:
Open all year.

Betws Road, Llanrwst, Conwy LL26 0PT
T: (01492) 642070
E: ralph@ffinyparc.co.uk **W:** www.ffinyparc.com

Ffin Y Parc Country House is set in 14 acres of parkland inside the Snowdonia National Park. Bedrooms are large, sophisticated and unique, with a mixture of antique and contemporary furnishings and original art. The downstairs boasts an art gallery that has twelve varied shows a year by some of Wales' leading contemporary artists. The licensed coffee-shop which is popular with visitors and locals alike, serves excellent tea and coffee, and a selection of cakes and light lunches all prepared by the owner. In the evenings it transforms into an elegant wine-bar! In addition there are two holiday cottages situated in converted outbuildings, suitable for couples or families, which are finished to the same high standard.

DINING: A selection of homemade cakes are served throughout the day. Light lunch is served between 1200–1430 (£5 - £12). On a Friday and Saturday night, simple suppers are served from 1900 in the conservatory or sandwiches in the lounge. (£7 - £18).

Site: ✿ P **Payment:** 💳 **Leisure:** ⚲ ▶ ☡ **Property:** 🐕 🖼 🗄 🎿 ✿ **Children:** 🐾 ⚲ **Catering:** ◖✕ ⛾ 🍴
Room: ⚲ 📺 📀

THE WEST ARMS HOTEL

Llanarmon Dyffryn Ceiriog, Near Llangollen, Denbighshire LL20 7LD
T: (01691) 600665 F: (01691) 600622
E: info@thewestarms.co.uk W: www.thewestarms.co.uk

The West Arms is a 16th century Inn, originally a farm owned by the family of Llangedwyn Hall, it later became a Drovers' Inn, and offers the same warmth and hospitality today as it did in 1570. Now owned by Geoff and Gill Leigh-Ford, they offer a very warm and professional welcome. This hotel is extremely old and very quaint with lots of little passageways, low ceilings and doors with plenty of snugs. The gardens are both spacious and well kept and have the sun on them for the best part of the day. West Arms is well and truly on the culinary map under the prowess of celebrity chef Grant Williams. The food is excellent, beautifully cooked, with flair and panache. His menus incorporate locally sourced food (Lady Kenyon of Greddington's home grown fruit and veg, Josh Williams' free range eggs, Dave Keegan of Llanrhaedr ym Mochant's Welsh lamb and beef, and Rosie Davies' edible flowers). Escape from a busy and stressful life and relax and enjoy the beauty of the Valleys.

DINING: Average main course £16, average starter £6, puddings £6. Open from 0800 until 2300: 1200-1430 and 1800-2100 meal times.

Site: P **Payment:** **Leisure:** **Property:** **Children:**
Catering: **Room:**

BEDROOMS: 16
All rooms unique, from the character rooms in the original part of the building to more contemporary rooms at the rear. All rooms offer clean comfort.

B&B PER ROOM PER NIGHT:
S: £45.00 - £115.00
D: £65.00 - £175.00

ADDITIONAL INFORMATION:
Explore the mountains and waterfalls nearby, with many local National Trust attractions close by, also pony trekking, horse riding, quad biking, white water rafting, Chester and Shrewsbury for shops.

Cymru Wales Tafarn Inn ★★★★ WALKERS WELCOME CYCLISTS WELCOME

See front of guide for key to symbols

TREFEDDIAN HOTEL

BEDROOMS: 59
Light, spacious and airy, all hotel rooms are en suite and include everything you'll need to feel at home, including TV, radio, direct dial telephone, tea and coffee making facilities and bath and/or shower.

B&B PER ROOM PER NIGHT:
S: £94.00 - £119.00
D: £188.00 - £276.00

ADDITIONAL INFORMATION:
Prices are inclusive of 5 course dinner, bed and breakfast. Open January to 6th December. Early and late season breaks available.

Aberdovey, Gwynedd LL35 0SB
T: (01654) 767213 **F:** (01654) 767777
E: info@trefwales.com **W:** www.trefwales.com

The Trefeddian Hotel in Aberdovey offers everything you could ask for from a family-friendly, fun-loving break in Mid Wales. Set in the rolling hills of the Snowdonia National Park, with panoramic views of the Mid Wales coast, it's a picture-perfect luxury bolthole. Stroll along the powder-soft sands of the Cambrian Coast, enjoy precious moments in our comfortable lounges, and discover your adventurous side on a trek of the rolling hills of the Snowdonia National Park. Then, enjoy a dip in our indoor pool, an afternoon tea on one of the terraces or some good, old-fashioned fun in the games room before retiring to one of our fifty-nine light, airy bedrooms, or winding down in a self-catering hideaway. With sweeping sea views, attentive service, and fine food cooked to perfection by our talented head chef, the dining room at the Trefeddian Hotel in Mid Wales is a delight for all the senses! The hotel's superb breakfast, lunch and 5 course table d'hôte menus are teeming with great local ingredients.

DINING: 5 course dinner £29.50; childrens' supper; lunch & special diets available; last orders 2100.

Site: P **Payment:** ⊞ **Leisure:** ♪ ▶ ♿ ⚿ ⚄ ✎ **Property:** ⋔ ▭ ▤ ⚄ ◑ **Children:** ⛞ ▥ ⚘
Catering: ⟨✗ ⚑ ⛾ **Room:** ⬇ ☎ TV ▨

Cymru
Wales
Tafarn
Inn
★★★

PALÉ HALL

Palé Estate, Llandderfel, Bala, Gwynedd LL23 7PS
T: (01678) 530285
E: enquiries@palehall.co.uk **W:** www.palehall.co.uk

Palé Hall is a delightful discovery for the discerning visitor – a lovingly restored Victorian country manor set in refreshingly tranquil and beautiful surroundings. Queen Victoria herself warmed to Palé's welcome during her visit in 1889 and her bath and bed are still in use today. The present family owners are proud to maintain the Hall's great tradition of hospitality. The elegance and grandeur of Palé remain unchanged while the amenities have been discreetly enhanced to the highest standards. We are sure Her Majesty would have approved. Palé Jewellers, based at the hotel, is a small but personal business devoted exclusively to Welsh gold jewellery from Cymru y Metal and Clogau Gold. The Hall lies in an unspoiled area of lush valleys and gentle hills, making it a paradise for outdoor activities: fishing, shooting, riding and mountaineering. Lake Bala, the largest natural lake in Wales (4½ miles long) is the only habitat of the trout-like gwyniaid. A steam railway runs alongside it.

DINING: Table d'hôte restaurant; lunch & special diets available; breakfast from 0800. The hotel is open to non-residents for meals.

Site: ❀ P **Payment:** 💳 **Leisure:** ♪ ♪ ♫ **Property:** ⬥ ☰ ⬛ ⬳ **Catering:** (✗ ☵ ⬚
Room: ⬚ ⬥ ☎ TV ⬚ ⬚

BEDROOMS: 17
Each individually apointed bedroom overlooks the grounds and bathrooms have been refurbished.

B&B PER ROOM PER NIGHT:
S: £90.00 - £155.00
D: £125.00 - £210.00

ADDITIONAL INFORMATION:
Open all year.

Single rates refer to single occupancy of a double room.

Other Facilities: Golf, fitness centre/gym, riding, shooting, watersports, sailing, 4x4 driving, croquet, helipad and wedding facilties.

BRON EIFION COUNTRY HOTEL

BEDROOMS: 18
All bedrooms are decorated in uniquely individual, yet classic styles. With comfortable beds Egyptian cotton sheets, comfy pillows and fluffy towels.

B&B PER ROOM PER NIGHT:
S: £95.00 - £185.00
D: £145.00 - £225.00

ADDITIONAL INFORMATION:
Visit Wales Gold Award 2015 - Ranked in AA Top 200 Hotels in the UK and Ireland.

Licensed for weddings.

Criccieth, Gwynedd LL52 0SA
T: (01766) 522385 **F:** (01766) 523796
E: enquiries@broneifion.co.uk **W:** www.broneifion.co.uk

The Bron Eifion Country House is a luxury 4 star hotel situated in Criccieth North Wales. This Grade II Listed building overlooks beautiful gardens with breathtaking views of the sea and is full of charm, warmth and genuine hospitality, offering the perfect venue for weekend breaks, weddings, conferences and meetings, water sport activities and of course golf. This historic house was built around 1883 and retains many of the original features offering visitors to Criccieth a unique experience combining luxury accommodation, fine dining and exceptional service. The hotel is ideally located on the Llyn Peninsula just a short walk from Criccieth and the beach, and an ideal destination for the keen golfer, boasting no less than five of North Wales' best golf courses nearby: Pwllheli, Nefyn, Abersoch, Royal St. David's Harlech, Porthmadog and Criccieth Golf Course quite literally on the doorstep.

DINING: AA rosette award winning restaurant. The restaurant is open each day for breakfast, lunch and dinner between 0730 and 2100.

Site: ❀ P **Payment:** 💳 **Leisure:** ♪ ▶ ♻ **Property:** ⊛ ♨ 🖼 🗄 🏨 🖉 **Children:** 🛝 🎠 🚸
Catering: (✕ 🍷 🍴 **Room:** 🗲 🐾 📞 🎧 📺

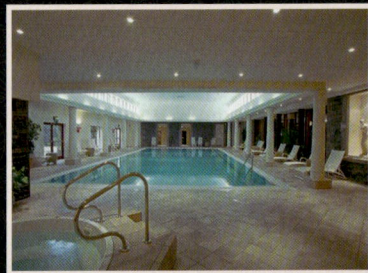

TRE-YSGAWEN HALL HOTEL & SPA

Capel Coch, Llangefni, Isle of Anglesey LL77 7UR
T: (01248) 750750 **F:** (01248) 750035
E: enquiries@treysgawen-hall.co.uk **W:** www.treysgawen-hall.co.uk

Reached along a private wooded drive, Tre-Ysgawen is set in 11 acres of landscaped gardens and woodland a short drive inland from the breathtaking East coast of Anglesey. The house has been sympathetically and luxuriously refurbished and extended to become one of the leading country house hotels in North Wales. Noëlle's offers a fine dining experience. The accent on Noëlle's is on using the best of seasonal local and regional produce. For a more relaxed dining experience there is The Clock Tower. Tre-Ysgawen Spa, built and equipped to the highest standards, was converted from the Victorian stables and retains many original features including the Clock Tower. Facilities include a 16m level-deck pool, salt inhalation therapy room, herbal essences sauna, ice fountain, spa bath, beauty/therapy suite and air-conditioned gymnasium.

DINING: Noëlles Restaurant, à la carte menu 1900 – 2130. Clock Tower Restaurant, bistro menu 1730 – 2130. Clock Tower daytime menu 0900 – 1700. 24 hour room service menu. Noëlles Bar menu serving times: 1700 - 2130 Sun - Thur and 1700 - 1900 Fri - Sat.

BEDROOMS: 29
Bedrooms in the main house are individually designed and decorated in traditional period style and while the rooms in the courtyard wing are more modern. Several of the bedrooms have been completely refurbished.

B&B PER ROOM PER NIGHT:
S: £118.00 - £176.00
D: £128.00 - £216.00

ADDITIONAL INFORMATION:
Open all year.

Site: ❀ **P** **Payment:** ▦ € **Leisure:** ♪ ▶ ∪ ☆ ⚲ ⚐ ⚘ **Property:** ⚑ ▤ ⚕ ◑ **Children:** ⚏ ▥ ⚐
Catering: (✕ ⚒ ⛾ **Room:** ⚐ ☁ ☎ ▣ 📺 ⚐ ⚐

GLEN YR AFON HOUSE HOTEL

BEDROOMS: 27

27 elegant bedrooms enjoy wonderfully large baths in which to luxuriate. Many bathrooms have been refurbished, along with the redecoration and refurbishment of bedrooms and public areas. Additionally there is Stable Cottage in the grounds for a bit more privacy!

B&B PER ROOM PER NIGHT:
S: £99.00 - £123.00
D: £136.00 - £150.00

ADDITIONAL INFORMATION:
Open all year. Leisure Breaks - Any two-night break, dinner, b&b for two sharing from £150 per person.

Pontypool Road, Llanbadoc, Monmouthshire NP15 1SY
T: (01291) 672302 **F:** (01291) 672597
E: enquiries@glen-yr-afon.co.uk **W:** www.glen-yr-afon.co.uk

The award-winning Glen-Yr-Afon House Hotel offers relaxation and a high level of personal service and attention, all in a rural location in the lovely county of Monmouthshire overlooking the banks of the River Usk. Only five minutes walk from the pleasant market town of Usk, this is a great base from which to explore South Wales, being only 15 minutes from the M50 and 10 minutes from the M4. Glen-Yr-Afon is an imposing and elegant Victorian house retaining many original features, yet sympathetically updated. Many of the guest bathrooms have benefited from recent refurbishment. Privately owned, the business opened its doors in March 1974. Glen-Yr-Afon's sister Hotel, The Three Salmons Hotel, a traditional coaching inn is just a 5 minute stroll into the town.

DINING: À la carte restaurant; special diets available; last orders 2145. Clarkes restaurant offers a range of new menu choices with an extensive wine list. Business people and wedding parties are well catered for with a function suite seating 150, whilst the charming Library is suitable for anniversaries, dinner parties and smaller functions for up to 20 people.

Site: ✿ P **Payment:** 💷 € **Leisure:** ♪ ⚑ ✂ **Property:** 🐕 ✕ ⛒ 🖥 🍴 ◐ **Children:** 🚼 ⚲
Catering: (✕ 🍷 🍽 **Room:** 🖥 🕯 📞 📶 📺 📀 🎛

AA ★★★ Hotel

WOLFSCASTLE COUNTRY HOTEL

Wolfscastle, Haverfordwest, Pembrokeshire SA62 5LZ
T: (01437) 741225 **F:** (01437) 741383
E: enquiries@wolfscastle.com **W:** www.wolfscastle.com

Wolfscastle is a friendly country house hotel and restaurant, formerly a vicarage, situated between Haverfordwest and Fishguard, just off the A40. It is still known locally by its original name Allt Yr Afon ('Wooded Hill by the River'). The stylish extension to the front has a cosy residents' lounge and brasserie style dining area. Wolfscastle's location and hospitality make it popular for conferences and weddings. It has been under the same ownership for over 35 years, and has gained a well deserved reputation for good food and friendly relaxed service, which will guarantee a memorable stay. Excellently located for exploring the Pembrokeshire Coast and National Park, the Preseli Hills and St David's – Britain's smallest cathedral city. Tregwynt Woollen Mill and a number of craft and pottery workshops are also nearby.

DINING: À la carte, 2 AA rosette restaurant. Lunch & special diets available. Last orders 2100. Breakfast from 0700.

BEDROOMS: 20
The 20 bedrooms, which have all been recently refurbished and fitted with 32" flat screen TVs, are either in the old vicarage part of the house or in the more modern rear part of the building.

B&B PER ROOM PER NIGHT:
S: £80.00 - £105.00
D: £120.00 - £145.00

ADDITIONAL INFORMATION:
Open all year.

Site: P Payment: 💳 **Property:** 🍷 🐾 🖥 📠 ⚧ ∅ **Children:** 🚼 🏠 ⚥ **Catering:** 🍴 🍷 🍽
Room: 🔌 ⚡ 📞 📺

WARPOOL COURT HOTEL

BEDROOMS: 22
The different style of bedrooms are named, the best Premier rooms having recently opened on the second floor. The walls of the Ramsey Room are decorated with nursery tiles and, lying in the bath of the Skomer Room, you can look out to Skomer Island.

B&B PER ROOM PER NIGHT:
S: £125.00 - £220.00
D: £145.00 - £340.00

ADDITIONAL INFORMATION:
Open 1st April - 1st November.

St Davids, Pembrokeshire SA62 6BN
T: (01437) 720300
E: info@warpoolcourthotel.com **W:** www.warpoolcourthotel.com

The Warpool Court is in a wonderful position overlooking the wild Atlantic and within a few minutes walk of the famous St. David's Cathedral. It is owned by Peter Trier, whose charming daughter Marianne helps the very professional and 'hands-on' manager Rupert Duffin. You can be assured of good food, gracious living and a warm welcome. The lounge bar, with its array of antique tiles, provides a relaxed atmosphere for that pre-dinner drink. The restaurant is open 7 days a week. There are numerous outdoor activities nearby and you can access the Pembrokeshire Coastal Path at one of its most dramatic stretches directly from the hotel's gardens. The restaurant has a high reputation for good food, backed by a fine selection of well chosen wines. The chef has many years' experience of tempting hotel guests and local diners, who come from a wide radius, to celebrate 'that special occasion' here.

DINING: Guests booking in advance for every night of stay £24.50pppn. Alternatively £39.50pppn; 3 courses with coffee. Lunch & special diets available; last orders 2115.

Site: ❀ P **Payment:** 💳 **Leisure:** ⚓ ♪ ▶ ♆ ⚲ ⚱ ⚹ **Property:** 🐾 ▦ ▣ ▨ ∅ **Children:** ⚶ ▥ ⚺
Catering: (✕ ♛ ▦ **Room:** ⚲ ⚱ ☎ 📺

PENALLY ABBEY COUNTRY HOUSE

Penally, Pembrokeshire SA70 7PY
T: (01834) 843033 F: (01834) 844714
E: info@penally-abbey.com W: www.penally-abbey.com

Penally Abbey is a fine country house rich in character and old world charm, a favourite with many celebrities. Standing in five acres of gardens and woodlands with magnificent views over Caldey Island and Carmarthen Bay, it exudes an air of peace and tranquillity that belies its monastic past. The hotel stands on the site of a 6th century abbey and there is a ruined medieval chapel and a wishing well in the garden. Larger and more individual bedrooms in the main Abbey House are individually and originally furnished with antiques, many having four posters. The coach house is an adjoining converted stable block resembling four stone cottages. Each has its own front door and is furnished in a cottage style. Dining is a romantic candle-lit affair, making use of the best seasonal local produce. There is a lot to see and do in this corner of Wales. Tenby has a sheltered harbour, Georgian and Regency houses, medieval castle ruins, town walls and a 13th century church. Tenby golf course is almost opposite the hotel and the Pembrokeshire Coastal Path passes nearby.

DINING: 3 course table d'hôte dinner non-residents £36. Special diets; last orders 2045.

Site: ❀ P Payment: 💳 Leisure: ♪ ↾ ∪ Property: ⌶ 🐾 🖿 ⊘ Children: ⊟ Catering: (✗ 🍴 🍽
Room: 🗠 🌡 📞 📺 🗄

BEDROOMS: 12
Individual rooms and The Coach House.

B&B PER ROOM PER NIGHT:
S: £112.50 - £176.00
D: £125.00 - £188.00

ADDITIONAL INFORMATION:
Single dinner b&b from £140. Double dinner, b&b from £206. Seabathing and shooting nearby.

LAKE VYRNWY HOTEL & SPA

BEDROOMS: 52
Every bedroom is individual in style with comfy beds and Egyptian cotton sheets. Choose from Garden view, Lake view or Premier Lake View rooms.

B&B PER ROOM PER NIGHT:
S: £124.00   £164.00
D: £149.00 - £269.00

ADDITIONAL INFORMATION:
Open all year.

Lake Vyrnwy, Llanwddyn, Mid Wales, Powys SY10 0LY
T: (01691) 870692 **F:** (01691) 870259
E: info@lakevyrnwyhotel.co.uk **W:** www.lakevyrnwy.com

Lake Vyrnwy Hotel and Spa is a multi-award-winning country house hotel in North Wales, with stunning views over unspoiled countryside and luxury four-star accommodation that makes it one of the finest hotels in Wales. Enjoy Lake Vyrnwy Hotel's own special kind of time travel; Spectacular views of Lake Vyrnwy and the iconic fairy-tale tower are timeless; and retain the character and feel of a Victorian country house. There are miles and miles of walks and trails to explore - they take you off the beaten track into the heart of the dramatic North Wales countryside. You will also discover North Wales' most luxurious spa to provide the ultimate pampering experience. However you spend your time at Lake Vyrnwy Hotel and Spa, you will enjoy yourself, relax and feel pampered… kick off your shoes if you want to - at Lake Vyrnwy Hotel we take a pride in high standards delivered with a comforting degree of informality.

DINING: Award winning Tower Restaurant offering a five course dinner at £39.95 (1845–2115); Tavern bistro offering a more informal dining experience (3 courses from £25) 1800–2100. Breakfast 0800–1000.

Site: ✿ P **Payment:** 💳 **Leisure:** ♪ ▶ ♦ ✕ ⨝ ⏣ ✎ **Property:** ⑧ ⓕ ♂ 🖃 🗐 ♨ ◑ ∅ **Children:** 🛏 🏠 ⚲
Catering: (✕ 🍴 🍲 **Room:** ⚲ ⚱ ☎ 🎧 TV DVD 🖾

MISKIN MANOR HOTEL & HEALTH CLUB

Miskin, Llantrisant, Nr Cardiff CF72 8ND
T: (01443) 224204 **F:** (01443) 237606
E: reservations@miskin-manor.co.uk **W:** www.miskin-manor.co.uk

Miskin Manor has a long history dating back to the 10th century. It was rebuilt in the 19th century along its present lines. In the war it was a hospital and after that was converted into flats. It became an hotel in 1986 and was bought by the Rosenberg family in 1997. The family and loyal staff have transformed it into one of the leading venues of South Wales, popular equally with business travellers not wishing to be in the city centre, leisure guests touring South Wales, wedding guests and conference planners. It sits in its own 25-acre parkland situated a short distance from Cardiff amongst spectacular gardens. The interior is baronial with moulded ceilings, oak panelling and chandeliers yet the attitude is friendly and inviting. There are three dining rooms serving award winning cuisine, locally sourced if possible, including Brecon venison and Welsh black beef.

DINING: AA 2 Rosette Meisgyn Restaurant à la carte 3 course ca £35; lunch & special diets available; last orders 2130; table d'hôte 2 course £17.95; 3 course £23.95. Breakfast from 0700.

BEDROOMS: 43
Bedrooms are spacious, many overlooking the gardens, which are triple winners of Wales in Bloom 2011, 2012 and 2013.

ADDITIONAL INFORMATION:
Open all year.

Single room with breakfast from £110; double from £155. Self-catering lodge, 2 x doubles available, please contact for rates.

Site: ❀ P **Leisure:** ▶ ∪ ✗ 🏊 ⚲ ❄ ✎ **Property:** ☂ 🐕 🖃 🖂 🅿 ◑ **Children:** ➤ **Catering:** ⟨✗ 🍴
Room: 🔲 🛏 ☏ 📺 📀 🖨

LOCATION MAPS

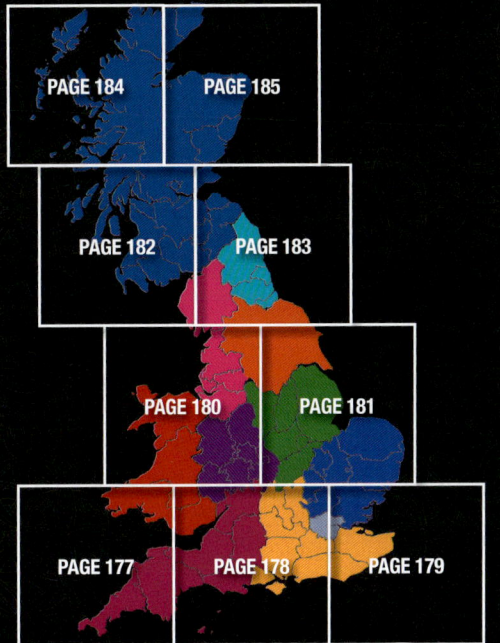

PAGE 184

PAGE 185

PAGE 182

PAGE 183

PAGE 180

PAGE 181

PAGE 177

PAGE 178

PAGE 179

Numbers in the magenta ovals on the following maps denote page numbers of Signpost approved hotels. Turn to these pages for full details of accommodation in the area where you are looking.

© Maidenhead Cartographic Ltd

Pembrokeshire Coast National Park
St. David's Head
Fishguard
Newport
Mathry
Mynydd Preseli
536
Llandovery
Llanwrda
CARMARTHENSHIRE
172
PEMBROKESHIRE
Carmarthen
Llandeilo
St. David's
173
Haverfordwest
Narberth
St. Clears
Ammanford
Ramsey Island
St. Brides Bay
Milford Haven
Neyland
Pendine
Kidwelly
Pontarddulais
Skomer I.
Pembroke Dock
174
Saundersfoot
Burry Port
M4
Pontardawe
Skokholm I.
Pembroke
Tenby
Llanelli
Neath
SWANSEA
St. Govan's Head
Carmarthen Bay
Gower
Worms Head
Port Talbot
The Mumbles
Swansea Bay
Porthcawl

Bristol Channel

Combe Martin
Lynton
Lynmouth
Ilfracombe
Woolacombe
Exmoor
Exmoor N. P.
Lundy
Braunton
Barnstaple
South Molton
Westward Ho!
Hartland Pt.
Clovelly
Bideford
Hartland
Great Torrington
Chulmleigh
DEVON
Bude
Holsworthy
Hatherleigh
Poundstock
Crediton
Okehampton
Boscastle
Launceston
Tintagel
Bovey Tracey
Port Isaac
Bodmin Moor
Dartmoor N. P.
Padstow
Ashburton
Wadebridge
Callington
Tavistock
Yelverton
Buckfastleigh
Bodmin
Liskeard
Saltash
Totnes
Newquay
PLYMOUTH
Ivybridge
St. Austell
Fowey
Looe
Torpoint
20
St. Agnes
Polperro
Kingsbridge
Redruth
Mevagissey
21
Truro
Salcombe
St. Ives
Camborne
Penryn
Prawle Point
Hayle
St. Mawes
St. Just
Marazion
Falmouth
Penzance
16
Helston
Land's End
Lizard Pt.
Lizard
17
CORNWALL

St. Martin's
Bryher
Tresco
Hugh Town
St. Mary's

0	10	20	30	40 kilometres
0		10		20	30 miles

Saffron Walden
Nayland
Felixstowe
Thaxted
Halstead
66
Harwich
67
Bishop's Stortford
Great Dunmow
Braintree
Colchester
The Naze
Sawbridgeworth
Witham
Marks Tey
Wivenhoe
Walton-on-the-Naze
Frinton-on-Sea
Harlow
Chelmsford
Kelvedon
Brightlingsea
Clacton-on-Sea
ESSEX
Mersea Island
Colne Point
Chipping Ongar
Maldon
Epping
Danbury
Chigwell
Billericay
Burnham-on-Crouch
Foulness Pt.
Brentwood
Wickford
Foulness I.
Basildon
Southend-on-Sea
City
Canvey Is.
Shoebury Ness
Tilbury
Grain
Thames Estuary
Dartford
Gravesend
Sheerness
Isle of Sheppey
Herne Bay
Margate
Swanley
Rochester
Gillingham
Broadstairs
Wrotham
Chatham
Sittingbourne
Whitstable
Ramsgate
MEDWAY
North Downs
Faversham
Sandwich
Sevenoaks
Maidstone
Chilham
Canterbury
Edenbridge
Tonbridge
KENT
Deal
Royal Tunbridge Wells
Staplehurst
Wye
Cranbrook
Ashford
Channel Tunnel Terminal
Dover
The Weald
Tenterden
Romney Marsh
Folkestone
Crowborough
Hythe
EAST
40
Uckfield
45
New Romney
Heathfield
Rye
Battle
Lydd
SUSSEX
43
Winchelsea
Dungeness
Lewes
Hailsham
Hastings
Strait of Dover
Polegate
Bexhill
42
Newhaven
Seaford
Eastbourne
Peacehaven
Beachy Head

E n g l i s h   C h a n n e l

CHANNEL ISLANDS
Alderney
Guernsey
Herm
St Peters Port
Sark
Jersey
28
St Helier

0   10   20   30   40 kilometres
0   10   20   30 miles

Isle of Man

A3 Ramsey
Peel A4 Laxey
A1 A5 Douglas
Port Erin A5 Castletown

Irish Sea

0 10 20 30 40 kilometres
0 10 20 30 miles

ANGLESEY ISLE
Amlwch
Holy Island Holyhead
Benllech
Valley **170** Beaumaris
Rhosneigr Menai Bridge
Llandudno Colwyn Bay **164** Rhyl
Prestatyn
Conwy Abergele Rhuddlan
St. Asaph Holywell
Bethesda Llanrwst **165** CONWY Denbigh
Caernarfon Capel Curig Betws-y-Coed Bylchau Mold FLINTSHIRE
Buckley
Snowdon 1085 Pentrefoelas Ruthin Llay Holt
Blaenau Ffestiniog DENBIGHSHIRE CHESHIRE
Ffestiniog Snowdonia Corwen Dee Llangollen Wrexham
Nefyn Lleyn Peninsula Bala Ruabon Overton
169 Criccieth Porthmadog **168** **166** Chirk Ellesmere
Pwllheli Trawsfynydd Bala Lake Whittington Wem
Harlech National Park Lake Vyrnwy Oswestry
Aberdaron Abersoch Tremadog Bay Dolgellau GWYNEDD **175** Llanfyllin
Bardsey Island Barmouth Llanfair Caereinion
Barmouth Bay Cader Idris 892 Mallwyd Welshpool Minsterley
167 Machynlleth Moelfre 468 Montgomery
Aberdovey Caersws Church Stretton
Borth Talybont Newtown Bishop's Castle
Cardigan Bay Aberystwyth Ponterwyd Llanidloes Craven Arms Clun
162 Devil's Bridge Llangurig Beacon Hill 547 Knighton Ludlow
Aberaeron New Quay Mynydd Bach 361 Llanbister Rhayader Penybont New Radnor Leominster
Aberporth CEREDIGION Tregaron Bryn Brawd 484 Drygarn Fawr 645 Llandrindod Wells Kington Weobley
Cardigan **163** Lampeter Builth Wells HEREFORDSHIRE
Newcastle Emlyn Llanybydder Llanwrtyd Wells Hay-on-Wye **96** Hereford
© Maidenhead Cartographic Ltd POWYS

Broughton-in-Furness **126** Kendal Sedbergh Askrigg Leyburn
Newby Bridge Kirkby Hawes Aysgarth NORTH YORKSHIRE
Millom **123** Cartmel Milnthorpe Lonsdale National Park Masham
Dalton-in-Furness Carnforth Ingleton Kettlewell Pateley Bridge
Barrow-in-Furness Morecambe Settle **111** Grassington
Isle of Walney Heysham Lancaster **113** Skipton Ilkley
Forest of Bowland Gisburn Keighley Otley Guiseley
Fleetwood LANCASHIRE Colne Bingley
Cleveleys Garstang Clitheroe Nelson Burnley Shipley BRADFORD
Thornton Longridge Todmorden Halifax Elland
BLACKPOOL Preston Darwen Rawtenstall Rochdale Ripponden Huddersfield
Lytham St. Anne's Kirkham Blackburn Bury Holmfirth
Southport Leyland Chorley Bolton Oldham
Formby Ormskirk Wigan Farnworth Peak District
Skelmersdale Kirkby Salford MANCHESTER Ashton-under-Lyne Glossop
Liverpool Bay Crosby St. Helens Urmston Stockport Chapel-en-le-Frith **81**
Wallasey LIVERPOOL Widnes Warrington Sale Cheadle
Hoylake Birkenhead Runcorn Altrincham Wilmslow Buxton
Heswall Neston Frodsham Knutsford Macclesfield Bakewell
Flint Helsby Northwich Middlewich **82**
Chester Tarporley Sandbach Biggin National Park
CHESHIRE Crewe Kidsgrove Leek Cheddleton
Nantwich Tunstall Ashbourne
Melpas STOKE-ON-TRENT Longton Cheadle
Whitchurch Woore Stone Uttoxeter Sudbury
99 Hodnet Market Drayton STAFFORDSHIRE
Shawbury Newport Stafford Rugeley
Shrewsbury Wellington **98** Dawley Shifnal Penkridge Cannock Lichfield
Telford M6 Toll Brownhills
Broseley Wolverhampton West Bromwich Tamworth Walsall
Much Wenlock Bridgnorth Dudley BIRMINGHAM
Wyre Forest Kidderminster Halesowen Solihull
Bewdley Stourport-on-Severn Bromsgrove
Tenbury Wells Redditch Droitwich Henley-in-Arden Alcester
Bromyard Worcester Stratford-upon-Avon
100 Great Malvern **101** Pershore Evesham Chipping Campden

SHROPSHIRE
Cambrian Mountains
Cardigan Bay
Caernarfon Bay

North Sea

NORTH YORKSHIRE
EAST RIDING OF YORKSHIRE
LINCOLNSHIRE
N.E. LINCS
DERBYSHIRE
NOTTINGHAMSHIRE
RUTLAND
LEICESTERSHIRE
NORTHANTS
CAMBRIDGESHIRE
NORFOLK
SUFFOLK
BEDFORDSHIRE
WARWICKS

National Park

Northallerton, Lastingham, Scalby, Scarborough, Bedale, Masham, Thirsk, Helmsley, Pickering, Filey, Hunmanby, Ripon, Boroughbridge, Malton, Norton, Bridlington, Knaresborough, Stamford Bridge, Yorkshire Wolds, Great Driffield, Harrogate, Wetherby, Pocklington, Hornsea, YORK, Tadcaster, Market Weighton, Beverley, LEEDS, Garforth, Riccall, Selby, South Cave, Cottingham, KINGSTON-UPON-HULL, Hedon, Withernsea, Castleford, Howden, Hessle, Patrington, Dewsbury, Knottingley, Goole, Wakefield, Pontefract, Crowle, Scunthorpe, Immingham, Grimsby, Spurn Head, Adwick le Street, Barnsley, Hatfield, Doncaster, Brigg, Cleethorpes, Penistone, Bentley, Epworth, Kirton-in-Lindsey, Caistor, North Somercotes, Rawmarsh, Stocksbridge, Rotherham, Bawtry, Market Rasen, SHEFFIELD, Maltby, Gainsborough, Louth, Mablethorpe, Dronfield, Worksop, Retford, Saxilby, Wragby, Alford, Stawley, Chesterfield, Lincoln, Ingoldmells, Clay Cross, Bolsover, Ollerton, Sutton-on-Trent, Bardney, Horncastle, Skegness, Matlock, Warsop, Mansfield, Woodhall Spa, Spilsby, Wirksworth, Alfreton, Southwell, Newark-on-Trent, Coningsby, Wainfleet All Saints, Belper, Ripley, Arnold, Cranwell, Wells-next-the-Sea, Brancaster, Blakeney, Sheringham, Cromer, Duffield, NOTTINGHAM, Bingham, Sleaford, Boston, The Wash, Hunstanton, Holt, North Walsham, DERBY, Ilkeston, Grantham, Heckington, Swineshead, Heacham, Burnham Market, Happisburgh, Burton-upon-Trent, Kegworth, Waltham-on-the-Wolds, Folkingham, Donington, Sandringham, Fakenham, Aylsham, Reepham, Swadlincote, Loughborough, Holbeach, Terrington St. Clement, King's Lynn, NORFOLK, Winterton-on-Sea, Ashby-de-la-Zouch, Mountsorrel, Melton Mowbray, Bourne, Spalding, The Fens, East Dereham, Norwich, Caister-on-Sea, Coalville, Syston, Oakham, Market Deeping, Crowland, Wisbech, Swaffham, Great Yarmouth, LEICESTER, Oadby, Rutland Water, Stamford, Thorney, Downham Market, Wymondham, Brundall, Atherstone, Enderby, Wigston, Uppingham, Duddington, Peterborough, March, Watton, Loddon, Barwell, Cosby, Corby, Oundle, Stilton, Whittlesey, Methwold, Mundford, Attleborough, Bungay, Beccles, Nuneaton, Hinckley, Market Harborough, Rothwell, Thrapston, Sawtry, Ramsey, Chatteris, Littleport, Brandon, Thetford, Harleston, Lowestoft, Bedworth, COVENTRY, Rugby, Naseby, Kettering, Huntingdon, Ely, Lakenheath, Diss, Halesworth, Southwold, Royal Leamington Spa, Irthlingborough, Raunds, Soham, Mildenhall, Eye, Warwick, Southam, Wellingborough, Rushden, Kimbolton, St. Ives, Histon, Burwell, Ixworth, Bury St. Edmunds, Saxmundham, Daventry, Northampton, Cambridge, Newmarket, Stowmarket, Framlingham, Wickham Market, Aldeburgh, Ettington, Byfield, Olney, Bedford, St. Neots, Great Shelford, Lavenham, Claydon, Woodbridge, Orford, Banbury, Towcester, Newport Pagnell, Kempston, Biggleswade, Melbourn, Haverhill, Clare, Hadleigh, Ipswich, Royston, Sudbury, BEDFORDSHIRE, Potton, SUFFOLK

A684, A19, A170, A1, A59, A64, A164, A166, A163, A61, A62, M62, M18, M180, M1, A57, A631, A156, A46, A15, A17, A52, A16, A151, A47, A1101, A1065, A134, A140, A143, A11, A14, A605, A427, A508, A45, A6, A5, A43, A428, A421, A606, A42, M45, M42, M6, A606

Scale: 0 10 20 30 40 kilometres / 0 10 20 30 miles

© Maidenhead Cartographic Ltd

Tiree

Lochaline
Salen
Mull
Craignure
Iona
Fionnphort
Ross of Mull
Kerrera
Seil
Luing
Scarba
Colonsay
Scalasaig
Oronsay
Ardlussa
Port
Askaig
Jura
Bowmore
Bridgend
Islay
Craighouse
Portnahaven
Ardbeg
Port Ellen
Gigha I.
Clachan
Lochranza
Knapdale
Tarbert
Sound of
Bute
Goatfell
874
Arran
Brodick
Lamlash
Holy
Island
Blackwaterfoot
Machrihanish
Bay
Machrihanish
Cnoc Moy
446
Mull of
Kintyre
Kintyre
Sanda
Island
Campbeltown
Rathlin
Island

Portnacroish
Loch
Etive
Connel
Oban
Taynuilt
Loch
Awe
Kilninver
Kilmelford
Inveraray
Lochgilphead
Tarbert
Tighnabruaich
Wemyss Bay
Bute
Rothesay
West Kilbride
Ardrossan
Saltcoats
Kilbrannan Sound

Rannoch Moor
Aberfeldy
Bridge of
Orchy
Loch Lyon
Kenmore
Dunkeld
Loch
Tay
Dalmally
Tyndrum
Killin
PERTH &
KINROSS
Crianlarich
Lochearnhead
Crieff
Ardlui
Loch Earn
151
Auchterarder
Queen Elizabeth
Forest Park
Callander
A9
Cairndow
Ben
154
Dunblane
Ochil Hills
Lomond
Aberfoyle
A84
Bridge of Allan
Luss
Target
974
Forth
Kippen
Stirling
Dollar
Garelochhead
Loch
150
Alloa
Argyll
Forest
Park
Helensburgh
Drymen
Bannockburn
M80
Grangemouth
Dunoon
Denny
Alexandria
Falkirk
Bo'ness
Greenock
Dumbarton
Milngavie
Linlithgow
Port Glasgow
Bishopbriggs
Cumbernauld
Bathgate
INVERCLYDE
Clydebank
Airdrie
Paisley
GLASGOW
Coatbridge
Johnstone
Beith
East
Hamilton
Motherwell
Dalry
Stewarton
Kilbride
Strathaven
SOUTH LANARKSHIRE
Kilwinning
Darvel
Lesmahagow
Stevenston
Carluke
Irvine
Galston
Lanark
Kilmarnock
Troon
Mauchline
EAST AYRSHIRE
Muirkirk
Abington
Prestwick
Ayr
Cumnock
Elvanfoot
New Cumnock
A76
145
Leadhills
Turnberry
Maybole
Sanquhar
Lowther Hills
Dalmellington
Moniaive
Thornhill
Girvan
SOUTH
AYRSHIRE
DUMFRIES AND
Galloway
Forest Park
Ballantrae
New Galloway
Dumfries
Loch Ken
Cairnryan
Newton Stewart
Castle Douglas
Dalbeattie
Stranraer
Glenluce
Wigtown
Gatehouse of
Fleet
Portpatrick
The Rhins
The
Machars
Kirkcudbright
Luce Bay
Port William
Whithorn
Wigtown Bay
Drummore
Burrow Head
Solway Firth
Mull of Galloway
Workington
Whitehaven
St. Bees Head
St. Bees
Egremont
Point of Ayre

0 10 20 30 40 kilometres
0   10   20   30 miles

Ailsa
Craig

144

© Maidenhead Cartographic Ltd

North
Sea

North

Sea

Perth **152**

EDINBURGH

Belford **136** Bamburgh

122

125

124

127

114

© Maidenhead Cartographic Ltd

© Maidenhead Cartographic Ltd

A964
Scapa
Flow
St. Mary's
Hoy
Burray
South
Ronaldsay
Pentland Firth
Burwick
Stroma
Scrabster
Duncansby Head
Thurso
John o' Groats
A836
Castletown
Dounreay
A882
A9
Wick
A897
A9
A99
Latheron
Kinbrace
Lybster
Helmsdale
Brora
Golspie
Dornoch Firth
Dornoch
Tarbat
Ness
Tain
Cromarty
Moray Firth
Lossiemouth
Burghead
Cullen
Portsoy
Rosehearty
Elgin
Buckie
Macduff
Fraserburgh
Nairn
A95
Banff
Fochabers
A98
A96
A941
Keith
Aberchirder
A950
A941
Rothes
Turriff
Mintlaw
MORAY
Forres
A90
Peterhead
Dufftown
Huntly
A947
Grantown-
on-Spey
ABERDEENSHIRE
Spey
A95
Ellon
Carrbridge
A938
Rhynie
Oldmeldrum
A96
Aviemore
Correen
Hills
Inverurie
A90
A9
Tomintoul
Kintore
A939
Alford
Glenmore
Forest Park
Dyce
Aberdeen
Cairngorm Mountains
Peterculter
A93
Aboyne
A93
Braemar
Ballater
Dee
Banchory
A93
Stonehaven
A92
Blair Atholl
Laurencekirk
Inverbervie
A9
153
ANGUS
Atholl
Brechin
Pitlochry
Kirriemuir
Montrose
Ballinluig

ORKNEY
ISLANDS
Papa Westray
Start Point
North Ronaldsay
Westray
Sanday
Rousay
Westray Firth
Eday
Sanday Sound
A966
Mainland
Stronsay
Stromness
Finstown
Shapinsay
A965
Kirkwall
Scapa
Flow
St. Mary's
Hoy
Burray
South
Ronaldsay
Burwick

0   10   20   30   40 kilometres
0   10   20   30 miles

HUDSONs
HISTORIC HOUSE & GARDEN
SHORT BREAKS

LAUNCHING HUDSON'S SHORT BREAKS
INSPIRING 3 DAY BREAKS EXPLORING STATELY HOMES & HISTORIC HOUSES

Hudson's and renowned travel experts, Martin Randall Travel, have teamed up to offer a new range of short break holidays. Come and discover some of the finest country houses and gardens in Britain, some famous, some less so, over 3 fascinating days. Your base is a comfortable hotel with a friendly welcome and you will be able to explore the history of Britain through great architecture, family stories, interior decoration and stunning works of art. The specialist knowledge of our expert guides will ensure you get the most of your visit as well as frequent glimpses behind the green baize door and time to take in spectacular gardens and landscaped parks.

www.hudsonsheritage.com/shortbreaks

INDEX

Hotels are listed alphabetically within their
region. Facilities are listed as a guide
only, please check with the hotel before
booking if you require specific facilities.

Hotel By Region & Special Features

♿ Disabled-Friendly Rooms*
▶ Golf available (on site or nearby)
🍷 Conference facilities
🏊 Swimming pool – outdoor or indoor
🐕 Dogs/pets accepted by arrangement
🐟 Fishing nearby
💍 Licensed for Civil Weddings*
🏋 Gym on site
✂ Health/beauty facilities on site

AREAS & HOTELS	PAGE	♿	▶	🍷	🏊	🐕	🐟	💍	🏋	✂
South West England										
Berry Head Hotel	18		✔	✔	✔	✔			✔	✔
Budock Vean Hotel on River	16		✔	✔	✔	✔		✔	✔	✔
Cottage (The)	21		✔	✔		✔				
Dart Marina Hotel (The)	19		✔		✔	✔	✔		✔	✔
Hannafore Point Hotel	17		✔	✔	✔	✔	✔		✔	✔
Inn at Fossebridge (The)	24		✔	✔		✔				✔
Lordleaze Hotel (The)	26			✔		✔				
Moorings Hotel (The)	28					✔				
Pear Tree at Purton (The)	27	✔	✔	✔		✔			✔	
Plantation House Hotel & Restaurant	20						✔			✔
Plumber Manor	23			✔		✔				
Queens Arms (The)	22	✔	✔	✔		✔				
White Hart Royal (The)	25	✔		✔		✔			✔	
South East England										
Cantley House Hotel	36			✔		✔			✔	✔
Deans Place Hotel	42			✔	✔	✔			✔	
Drakes Hotel	44			✔						
Flackley Ash Hotel	45	✔		✔	✔	✔			✔	✔
Mill House Hotel & Restaurant	41			✔		✔				
Millstream Hotel	46			✔						
Montagu Arms Hotel	37	✔		✔			✔		✔	
PowderMills Hotel	43			✔	✔					
Priory Bay Hotel (The)	39	✔		✔	✔	✔	✔		✔	✔
Romney Bay House	40	✔		✔						
White Horse Hotel (The)	38			✔		✔				
London										
Mayflower (The)	56									
New Linden (The)	58									
San Domenico House	55									
Searcys Roof Garden Rooms	54			✔						
Twenty Nevern Square	57			✔						

* Symbols do NOT appear on entry pages.

- ♿ Disabled-Friendly Rooms*
- ▶ Golf available (on site or nearby)
- 🍸 Conference facilities
- 🏊 Swimming pool – outdoor or indoor
- 🐕 Dogs/pets accepted by arrangement
- 🐟 Fishing nearby
- 💒 Licensed for Civil Weddings*
- 🏋 Gym on site
- 🍴 Health/beauty facilities on site

AREAS & HOTELS	PAGE	♿	▶	🍸	🏊	🐕	🐟	💒	🏋	🍴
East of England										
Broom Hall Country Hotel	69			✔	✔	✔				
Hintlesham Hall Hotel	70		✔	✔		✔				✔
Maison Talbooth	66	✔	✔	✔	✔	✔	✔	✔	✔	✔
Milsoms Kesgrave Hall	71	✔	✔	✔		✔		✔		
Norfolk Mead Hotel (The)	68		✔	✔	✔	✔	✔			
Pier at Harwich	67	✔	✔	✔		✔		✔		
East Midlands										
Barnsdale Lodge Hotel	88		✔	✔		✔				✔
Biggin Hall Hotel	82			✔		✔	✔			
Cavendish Hotel (The)	80		✔	✔						
Langar Hall	87		✔	✔		✔	✔			
Losehill House Hotel & Spa	81		✔	✔	✔	✔			✔	✔
Manners Arms	83			✔		✔				
Talbot Hotel (The)	85	✔	✔	✔		✔		✔		
Washingborough Hall Hotel	84			✔		✔		✔		
Whittlebury Hall Hotel and Spa	86		✔							✔
Heart of England										
Castle House	96					✔	✔			
Chase Hotel (The)	97		✔	✔						
Cottage in Wood	100		✔	✔		✔				
Eckington Manor	101			✔						
Mytton & Mermaid Hotel	98			✔		✔				
Soulton Hall	99			✔						
Yorkshire										
Coniston Hotel (The)	113		✔	✔		✔	✔			
Feversham Arms Hotel & Verbena Spa	110			✔	✔	✔				✔
Lastingham Grange Country House Hotel	112		✔			✔	✔			
Raithwaite Estate	114	✔	✔	✔	✔	✔	✔		✔	✔
Sportsmans Arms Hotel & Restaurant	111					✔	✔		✔	

* Symbols do NOT appear on entry pages.

Key:
- ♿ Disabled-Friendly Rooms*
- ▶ Golf available (on site or nearby)
- 🍸 Conference facilities
- 🏊 Swimming pool – outdoor or indoor
- 🐕 Dogs/pets accepted by arrangement
- 🎣 Fishing nearby
- 💒 Licensed for Civil Weddings*
- 🤸 Gym on site
- 💆 Health/beauty facilities on site

AREAS & HOTELS	PAGE	♿	▶	🍸	🏊	🐕	🎣	💒	🤸	💆
North West England										
Aynsome Manor Hotel	123					✔				
Borrowdale Gates Hotel	125	✔	✔			✔	✔			
Gilpin Hotel & Lake House	126		✔				✔		✔	
Holbeck Ghyll Country House Hotel	127		✔	✔		✔			✔	✔
Lovelady Shield Country House Hotel	122		✔	✔		✔	✔			
Oak Bank Hotel	124		✔			✔	✔		✔	
North East England										
Waren House Hotel	136		✔			✔				
Scotland										
Atholl Palace Hotel, Spa & Lodges	153			✔	✔				✔	
Blackaddie Country House Hotel	145		✔	✔		✔	✔			
Duisdale House Hotel	148			✔		✔	✔	✔		
Eddrachilles Hotel	146					✔				
Four Seasons Hotel (The)	151		✔	✔		✔	✔			
Loch Melfort Hotel	144		✔	✔		✔	✔			
Murrayshall Hotel & Golf Courses	152	✔	✔	✔		✔		✔		
Roman Camp Country House Hotel	154		✔	✔		✔	✔			
Toravaig House Hotel	149					✔	✔		✔	
Viewfield House	147		✔			✔	✔			
Winnock Hotel (The)	150		✔	✔			✔			
Wales										
Bron Eifion Country Hotel	169		✔	✔			✔			
Falcondale Hotel and Restaurant (The)	163		✔	✔		✔				
Ffin y Parc Country House	165		✔			✔				
Glen Yr Afon House Hotel	171		✔	✔		✔	✔	✔		
Lake Vyrnwy Hotel & Spa	175		✔	✔		✔	✔		✔	✔
Miskin Manor Country Hotel	176		✔	✔	✔	✔		✔	✔	✔
Nanteos Mansion	162	✔	✔	✔		✔	✔	✔		✔
Palé Hall	168		✔	✔			✔			
Penally Abbey Country House	174		✔	✔		✔	✔			
St Tudno Hotel	164		✔			✔				
Trefeddian Hotel	167		✔		✔	✔	✔			✔
Tre-Ysgawen Hall Hotel & Spa	170		✔	✔	✔		✔		✔	✔
Warpool Court Hotel	173		✔		✔	✔	✔			
West Arms Hotel (The)	166	✔	✔	✔		✔	✔	✔		
Wolfscastle Country Hotel	172			✔		✔				

* Symbols do NOT appear on entry pages.

HUDSON'S MEDIA LIMITED

Published by:
Hudson's Media Ltd
35 Thorpe Road,
Peterborough, PE3 6AG
Tel: 01733 296910
Fax: 01733 209292

Hotel Inspectors: Gary Swarbrooke, Malcolm Orr-Ewing, Paul Riley, Casper Swinley, Steve Johnston, Ranald Duff

Editor: Deborah Coulter
Production team: Deborah Coulter, Rhiannon McCluskey, Rebecca Owen-Fisher

Creative: Jamieson Eley

Production System: NVG – leaders in Tourism Technology. www.nvg.net

Printer: Stephens & George, Merthyr Tydfil

Maps: Maidenhead Cartographic Services Ltd.

Retail Sales: Compass
Tel: 020 8996 5764

Photography credits: © Abbotsbury Subtropical Gardens, Alnwick Castle, Althorp, Athelhampton House, Balmoral Castle, Bamburgh Castle, Beamish Museum, Belvoir Castle, Blair Castle, Blenheim Palace, Bodleian Library, Bolton Castle, Britain on View, Browsholme, Burghley, Burton Agnes Hall, Castle Ashby Gardens, Castle Howard, Chatsworth, Cholmondeley Castle, Clovelly, Commons.Wikimedia.org, Coworth Park, The Coniston Hotel, Deborah Coulter, Eastnor Castle, The Eden Project, Elton Hall, English Heritage, Exbury Gardens/Dave Zubraski, Feversham Arms, Fonmon Castle, Gregynog, Haddon Hall, Harewood House, Hergest Croft Gardens, Hever Castle, Highclere Castle, Historic Royal Palaces/Kensington Palace, Holker Hall, Holkham Hall, Inveraray Castle, Knebworth House/Robert Smith, Lamport Hall, Leeds Castle, Levens Hall, Mount Stuart, Muncaster Castle, Pashley Manor Gardens/Helen Sinclair, Powdermills, Scampston, Sherborne Castle, Skipton Castle, Somerleyton Hall, Spencer House, Sudeley Castle, The Alnwick Garden, The Forbidden Corner, VisitEngland, Welcome to Yorkshire, Weston Park, Woburn Abbey.

© VisitBritain Images: Adam Burton, Andrew Pickett, Arnhel de Serra, Ben Selway, County Durham Tourism Partnership, Craig Easton, Daniel Bosworth, Eric Nathan, Grant Pritchard, Harry Williams, Ian Shaw, Jason Hawkes, Joe Cornish, Lee Beel, Martin Brent, Pawel Libera, Rod Edwards, Simon Winnall, Tony Pleavin.

ISBN 978-0-85101-560-6